BLOOM

Founded by | arihant

Olympiad ACE

A Comprehensive Practice Book

for School Olympiads & Talent Search Exams

SOCIAL STUDIES

Class 6

by

Adhishree Neurgaonkar

Olympiad ACE

BLOOM
Bloom Cap Edu Ventures Pvt. Ltd.

卐 **Administrative & Production Office**

'Ramchhaya' 4577/15, Agarwal Road, Darya Ganj, New Delhi -110002
Tele: 011- 47630600, 43518550

卐 **PRICE:** ₹125.00

Published by Arihant Publications (I) Ltd.

For further information about the books log on to
www.bloomcap.org

Follow us on

Preface

"Future belongs to those Who prepares for it today"

School Olympiads are National & International level competitions conducted by different Government, Non-Government & Educational Organisations with the purpose of making the children ready to face competitive exams.

The challenging Questions asked in Olympiads motivate them to learn more & more and bring out the best results with improved academic performance. The Awards & Scholarship offered by Olympiads motivate children to aspire & strive for doing better and emerge out to be the best.

Social Studies Olympiads

Social Studies provides students with a comprehensive understanding of society, politics, economics and history. Studying Social Studies helps students understand the complexities of society, and prepares them for careers in fields such as public service, education, law, journalism, and research.

Social Studies Olympiads are meant to develop students' interest towards this vital subject.

'Bloom Social Studies Olympiad Study Book Class 6' is a perfect resource to Study & Practice for Olympiad Exams and other National & State Level Talent Search Exams & Other Competitions.

Some Special Features of Bloom Social Studies Olympiad Study Books are;

- Complete coverage of all the aspects of History, Geography and Civics.
- Chapterwise Exercises having different types of Objective Questions at par with the Olympiad Level.
- Olympiad Pattern Practice Sets at the end.

This book is prepared by Expert Panel with the utmost care, still if you have any suggestions regarding its improvement then feel free to contact us at support@bloomcap.org. We will try to inculcate your suggestions in the further editions.

Contents

Chapter

01

The Study of the Past

MCQs 1 Mark Questions

1. The study of events, people and their way of living in past is known as ....

(a) History (b) Civics
(c) Geography (d) Political Life

2. Sulaiman and Kirthar Hills in .... of India were a region where women and men first began to grow crops such as wheat and barley about 8000 years ago.

(a) North-East (b) South-East
(c) North-West (d) South-West

3. Which of the following rivers is a tributary of Son River?

(a) Narmada (b) Ganga
(c) Indus (d) Yamuna

4. The ancient kingdom Magadha now comprises of which of the following state of India?

(a) Uttar Pradesh (b) Jharkhand
(c) Madhya Pradesh (d) Bihar

5. .... were usually written by hand on palm leaves or on bark of birch trees from Himalayas.

(a) Scripts
(b) Manuscripts
(c) Inscriptions
(d) Vedas

6. Which of the following statements is/are true?

(a) Most of the early human beings live on the banks of river.
(b) They collected roots, fruits and other items from forests.
(c) For the first time, rice was grown in Northern Vindhyas range.
(d) All of the above

7. In which language(s) were the manuscripts written during the earlier times?

(a) Sanskrit and Prakrit
(b) Hindi and Arabic
(c) Tamil
(d) Both (a) and (c)

8. Identify the source on which the rules and orders of the Kings and information about their Kingdom can be found.

(a) Manuscripts (b) Inscriptions
(c) Royal Decree (d) Paper Rolls

9. Choose the correct chronological order of the given texts.

(a) Vedas, Ramayana, Panchatantra, Arthashastra
(b) Arthashastra, Ramayana, Vedas, Panchatantra
(c) Ramayana, Vedas, Arthashastra, Panchatantra
(d) Vedas, Panchatantra, Arthashastra, Ramayana

10. The inscription given below dates to about 2250 years ago and was found in Kandahar, present-day Afghanistan. It was written on the orders of a ruler named ....

(a) Bimbisara (b) Ashoka
(c) Chandragupta Maurya (d) Ajatshatru

11. Pick the odd one out.
(a) Mahabharata (b) Ramayana
(c) Upanishads (d) Indika

12. Look at the given picture of a pot from an old city. Pots like these were used about .... ago.

(a) 2500 years (b) 3000 years
(c) 4500 years (d) 4700 years

13. Identify the incorrect statement regarding the importance of historical sources.
(a) It helps the historians in the reconstruction of our past.
(b) It provides information about the Kings and their measures.
(c) It helps to gather information about different occupations of people of our past.
(d) None of the above

14. Fa Hein and Hiuen Tsang who came to study Buddhism in India belonged to which of the following countries?
(a) Turkey (b) Japan
(c) China (d) France

15. Dates in history are expressed in two terms that are ....
(a) BC and AD (b) BC and BCE
(c) BCE and CE (d) Both (a) and (c)

16. What is the full form of AD?
(a) Active Directory (b) Anno Domini
(c) After Dawn (d) Active Domini

17. The letters BC stands for ....
(a) Before Christ
(b) Basic Christ
(c) Before Correspondent
(d) Basic Channel

MCQs 2 Marks Questions

Directions (Q. 18-19) Look at the map given below and answer the following questions.

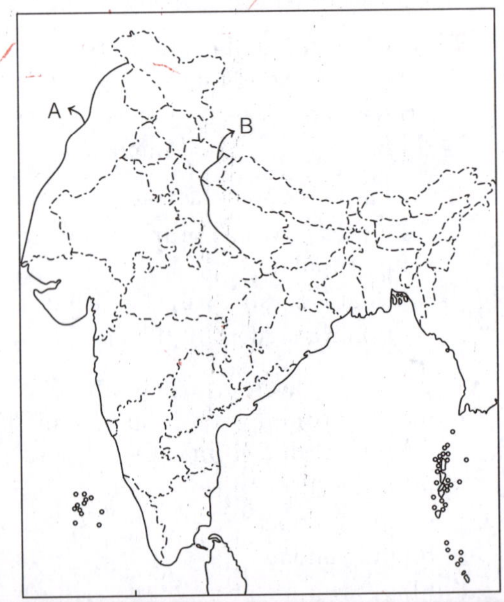

18. Which amongst the following is the river marked with 'A' in the above map?

(a) Indus (b) Ganga
(c) Brahmaputra (d) Jhelum

19. Which amongst the following is the river marked with 'B' in the above map?

(a) Indus (b) Yamuna
(c) Ganga (d) Narmada

20. Consider the following statements regarding literary sources for construction of history.

I. Text such as Ramayana, Angas and Tripitakas help to understand religious beliefs and practices.

II. Panchatantra, Manusmriti are the examples of secular literature.

III. Harshacharita, the biography of Harshavardhana is written by Banabhatta.

Choose the correct statements from the options given below.

(a) I and II (b) II and III
(c) I and III (d) I, II and III

21. Which of the following statements is/are incorrect regarding the archaeologists?

(a) They study the remains of buildings made of stone and brick, paintings and sculpture.

(b) They explore and excavate to find tools, weapons, coins, etc.

(c) They analyse and interpret historical information to determine its authenticity and significance.

(d) Both (a) and (b)

22. Choose the correct statements about writing inscriptions on the hard surface such as on backed clay, stone or metal during the earlier period.

(a) These objects were imperishable thus these writings usually survived for a long time.

(b) These objects were easily accessible.

(c) These objects were meant for writing inscriptions during those times.

(d) Both (a) and (b)

23. There are two statements marked as Assertion (A) and Reason (R). Mark your answer as per the codes given below.

Assertion (A) Past of Kings and Kingdoms can be known whereas past of common folks, hunters, gatherers is still unknown.

Reason (R) Kings kept the records of their lives and battles through inscriptions whereas ordinary people did not keep the records of what they did.

Codes

(a) Both A and R are true and R is the correct explanation of A

(b) Both A and R are true, but R is not the correct explanation of A

(c) A is true, but R is false

(d) A is false, but R is true

Darken your choice with HB Pencil

1.	(a) (b) (c) (d)	5.	(a) (b) (c) (d)	9.	(a) (b) (c) (d)	13.	(a) (b) (c) (d)	17.	(a) (b) (c) (d)	21.	(a) (b) (c) (d)
2.	(a) (b) (c) (d)	6.	(a) (b) (c) (d)	10.	(a) (b) (c) (d)	14.	(a) (b) (c) (d)	18.	(a) (b) (c) (d)	22.	(a) (b) (c) (d)
3.	(a) (b) (c) (d)	7.	(a) (b) (c) (d)	11.	(a) (b) (c) (d)	15.	(a) (b) (c) (d)	19.	(a) (b) (c) (d)	23.	(a) (b) (c) (d)
4.	(a) (b) (c) (d)	8.	(a) (b) (c) (d)	12.	(a) (b) (c) (d)	16.	(a) (b) (c) (d)	20.	(a) (b) (c) (d)		

Chapter 02

The Early Human Beings

MCQs 1 Mark Questions

1. Which of the following remains have survived for the longest time which was used by the early human beings?
   (a) Wood (b) Stone tools
   (c) Bones (d) All of these

2. Identify the purposes for which stone tools was/were used.
   (a) To cut meat and bones
   (b) To scrape bark from trees
   (c) To make spears and arrows for hunting
   (d) All of the above

3. Why did the early human beings lead a nomadic life?
   (a) Due to limited available resources.
   (b) Due to the movement of animals from one place to another on which humans hunted.
   (c) Due to search of water bodies such as rivers or lakes.
   (d) All of the above

4. Bhimbetka, which is famous for its rock cave shelters is located in ....
   (a) Uttar Pradesh (b) Rajasthan
   (c) Madhya Pradesh (d) Maharashtra

5. In which of the following places traces of ash have been found in India?
   (a) Kurnool Caves (b) Ajanta Caves
   (c) Bhimbetka Caves (d) Udyagiri Caves

6. Rock shelters are close to which of the following valleys?
   (a) Narmada Valley
   (b) Chenab Valley
   (c) Brahmaputra Valley
   (d) Kangra Valley

7. Rock paintings show wild animals, drawn with great accuracy and skill. Where are these paintings are mainly found?
   (a) Maharashtra and Uttarakhand
   (b) Madhya Pradesh and Southern Uttar Pradesh
   (c) West Bengal and Assam
   (d) Karnataka and Maharashtra

8. Identify the types of stone tools found during the Mesolithic period which were generally tiny known as Microliths.
   (a) Saws and sickles (b) Stone scrapers
   (c) Hand adzes (d) Cleavers

9. Which of the following crops started growing in different parts of world during Paleolithic period?
   (a) Wheat (b) Rice
   (c) Barley (d) All of these

10. Which amongst the following was the first tamed animal by the humans in the earliest period?
    (a) Elephant (b) Dog
    (c) Cow (d) Horse

11. Huts, cooking hearths, pit houses which were used by the earliest human beings were found in which modern day region of India?

(a) Kashmir
(b) Madhya Pradesh
(c) Gujarat
(d) Karnataka

12. What conclusion(s) can be drawn based on the findings from Burzahom?

(a) Pit houses were used to provide shelter from cold and extreme weather.
(b) Depending on the weather, people cooked food either inside or outside of the huts.
(c) Number of various crops were grown in earlier period.
(d) All of the above

13. Catal Huyuk settlement lies in which of the following countries?

(a) Turkey
(b) Afghanistan
(c) India
(d) Iran

14. Which of the following remains have been recovered from settlement of Catal Huyuk?

(a) Flints (b) Cowries
(c) Shells (d) All of these

15. From which of the following sites remains of square or rectangular houses were founds?

(a) Mehrgarh (b) Burzahom
(c) Chirand (d) Hallur

16. Identify the pass which links India with Iran from the given options.

(a) Jelep Pass
(b) Bolan Pass
(c) Khyber Pass
(d) Lipu-Lekh Pass

MCQs 2 Marks Questions

Directions (Q. 17-18) Look at the map given below and answer the following questions.

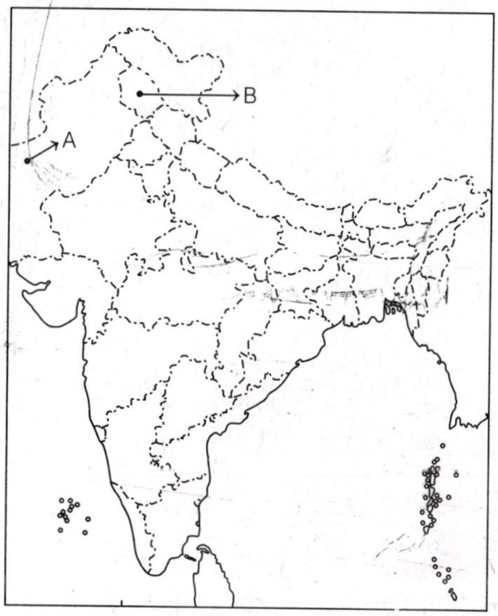

17. Which of the following sites is marked with 'A' in the above map?

(a) Mehrgarh
(b) Burzahom
(c) Rakhigarhi
(d) Kalibangan

18. Which of the following sites is marked with 'B' in the above map?

(a) Dholavira
(b) Mehrgarh
(c) Kalibangan
(d) Burzahom

19. Read the following statements and select which ones are true (T) and which ones are false (F).

I. Excavations at Kurnool Caves suggest that people earlier were familiar with the use of fire.
II. Sites may be found on the surface of the Earth, buried under the Earth or sometimes even under water.

III. Around 12000 years ago, there was climatic change. The temperature became cold which led to development of cold deserts.

Codes

	I	II	III		I	II	III
(a)	T	T	T	(b)	F	T	T
(c)	T	T	F	(d)	F	F	T

20. Match the following.

List I (Raw materials)	List II (States)
A. Tin	1. Afghanistan
B. Copper	2. Rajasthan
C. Gold	3. Karnataka
D. Precious stones	4. Iran

Codes

	A	B	C	D		A	B	C	D
(a)	1	2	3	4	(b)	2	3	1	4
(c)	3	1	4	2	(d)	4	2	1	3

21. Read the passage given below and fill in the blanks by choosing correct options given below.

.....(A)..... is located in fertile near Bolan pass and is one of the most important routes to Iran. It was one of the places where people learnt to grow .....(B)..... and wheat.

	A	B
(a)	Mehrgarh	barley
(b)	Lothal	corn
(c)	Kalibangan	rice
(d)	Dholavira	wheat

22. There are two statements marked as Assertion (A) and Reason (R). Mark your answer as per the codes given below.

Assertion (A) Kurnool is a city in Maharashtra which is known for its Paleolithic era cave paintings.

Reason (R) Traces of ash have been found here which suggests people were familiar with the use of fire. The city is located on Tungabhadra river.

Codes

(a) Both A and R are true and R is the correct explanation of A

(b) Both A and R are true, but R is not the correct explanation of A

(c) A is true, but R is false

(d) A is false, but R is true

23. Consider the following statements.

I. Number of Paleolithic sites have been found in Hunsgi, situated in Yadgiri district of Karnataka.

II. Tools found in Paleolithic period included longish blades with sharp edges and many multi-purposes instruments.

Choose the correct statement(s) from the codes given below.

(a) Only I
(b) Only II
(c) Both I and II
(d) Neither I nor II

Darken your choice with HB Pencil

1. ⓐ ⓑ ⓒ ⓓ	5. ⓐ ⓑ ⓒ ⓓ	9. ⓐ ⓑ ⓒ ⓓ	13. ⓐ ⓑ ⓒ ⓓ	17. ⓐ ⓑ ⓒ ⓓ	21. ⓐ ⓑ ⓒ ⓓ
2. ⓐ ⓑ ⓒ ⓓ	6. ⓐ ⓑ ⓒ ⓓ	10. ⓐ ⓑ ⓒ ⓓ	14. ⓐ ⓑ ⓒ ⓓ	18. ⓐ ⓑ ⓒ ⓓ	22. ⓐ ⓑ ⓒ ⓓ
3. ⓐ ⓑ ⓒ ⓓ	7. ⓐ ⓑ ⓒ ⓓ	11. ⓐ ⓑ ⓒ ⓓ	15. ⓐ ⓑ ⓒ ⓓ	19. ⓐ ⓑ ⓒ ⓓ	23. ⓐ ⓑ ⓒ ⓓ
4. ⓐ ⓑ ⓒ ⓓ	8. ⓐ ⓑ ⓒ ⓓ	12. ⓐ ⓑ ⓒ ⓓ	16. ⓐ ⓑ ⓒ ⓓ	20. ⓐ ⓑ ⓒ ⓓ	

Chapter 03

The Early Cities

MCQs 1 Mark Questions

1. The Harappan cities were divided into two or more smaller parts with usually Western part lower than Eastern part. Such parts were named by Archaeologists as ....

(a) town (b) citadel

(c) area (d) compartments

2. Which of the following was the most important and giant remain found in Mohenjodaro?

(a) Bullock carts (b) Great bath

(c) Dockyard (d) Bead makers shop

3. Complete the given analogy.

Harappa : Elaborate stone houses : : ? : Fire Altars

(a) Mohenjodaro (b) Banawali

(c) Kalibangan (d) Dholavira

4. Archaeologists have found a set of unique objects in almost all the Harappan cities. Identify the object(s) from the given options.

(a) Copper tools

(b) Paralleled sided long stone blades

(c) Marble tools

(d) Both (a) and (b)

5. The picture given below is of a bronze statue discovered from one of the Harappan site. Identify the site.

(a) Harappa

(b) Lothal

(c) Mohenjodaro

(d) Rakhigarhi

6. Which of the following metals was/were used to make ornaments, tools, weapons and vessels in the early Harappan cities?

(a) Copper

(b) Iron

(c) Bronze

(d) Both (a) and (c)

7. Identify the colour designs which were usually found on the pottery in Harappan Civilisation.
(a) Green designs (b) Blue designs
(c) Black designs (d) Red designs

8. Traces of cultivation of which of the following crops had been found in Mehrgarh?
(a) Jute (b) Wheat
(c) Rice (d) Cotton

9. Actual pieces of cloth attached to the lid of silver vase and other copper objects were found in ....
(a) Harappa (b) Kalibangan
(c) Lothal (d) Mohenjodaro

10. From where did Harappans import copper?
(a) Rajasthan and Oman
(b) Gujarat and Oman
(c) Gujarat and Iran
(d) Afghanistan

11. Harappans obtain Gold during Harappan Civilisation from which of the following states?
(a) Karnataka (b) Rajasthan
(c) Tamil Nadu (d) Gujarat

12. The picture given below shows beads which were generally made from a particular semi-precious stones. Identify the stone from the given options.

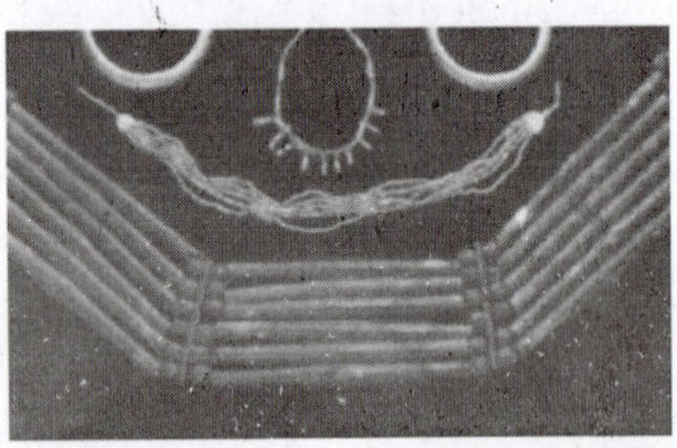

(a) Amazonite (b) Carnelian
(c) Copper (d) Terracotta

13. Which was the only ancient Harappan city that was divided into three parts?
(a) Harappa (b) Kalibangan
(c) Dholavira (d) Rakhigarhi

14. In which direction was the head of the dead person while burying in Inamgaon?
(a) North (b) South (c) East (d) West

MCQs 2 Marks Questions

Directions (Q. 15-16) Look at the map of India given below and answer the following questions.

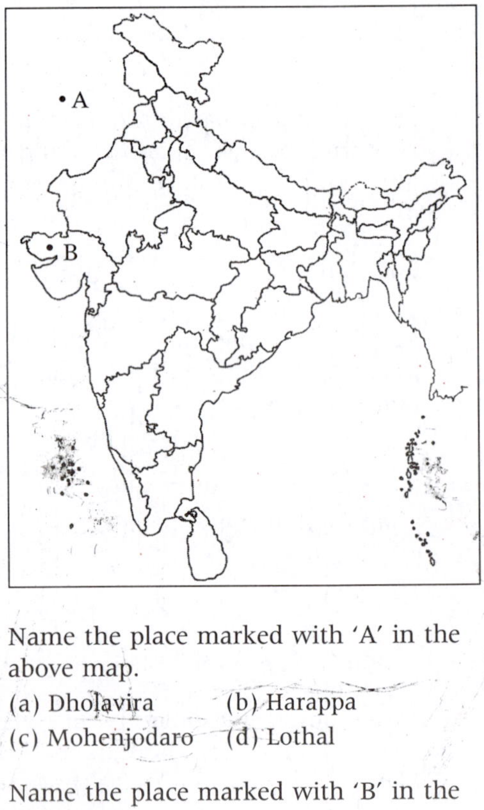

15. Name the place marked with 'A' in the above map.
(a) Dholavira (b) Harappa
(c) Mohenjodaro (d) Lothal

16. Name the place marked with 'B' in the above map.
(a) Lothal
(b) Dholavira
(c) Rakhigarhi
(d) Kalibangan

17. Which of the following statements is incorrect about the Harappan cities?

(a) Most houses had a separate bathing area and some had wells to supply water.

(b) Many of the cities had covered drains.

(c) There were people who planned the construction of special buildings in the city.

(d) The city was governed by the Harappan people instead of rulers.

18. There are two statements marked as Assertion (A) and Reason (R). Mark your answer as per the codes given below.

Assertion (A) People in Indus Valley knew the art of writing and developed the script.

Reason (R) Indus Valley script was pictographic and had picture like objects.

Codes

(a) Both A and R are true and R is the correct explanation of A

(b) Both A and R are true, but R is not the correct explanation of A

(c) A is true, but R is false

(d) A is false, but R is true

19. Identify the city from the information given below.

- It was the port city of Harappan Civilisation.
- Rice husks, bead makers shop were found in this city.

(a) Dholavira

(b) Lothal

(c) Kalibangan

(d) Rakhigarhi

20. Read the following passage and answer the question.

Inamgaon is a megalithic site. It was occupied between 3600 and 2700 years ago. Bones of a number of animals, many bearing cut marks that show they may have been used as food, have also been found.

Which of the following animals was not domesticated by people of Inamgaon?

(a) Cattle

(b) Dog

(c) Cat

(d) Horse

Darken your choice with HB Pencil

1.	ⓐ ⓑ ⓒ ⓓ	5.	ⓐ ⓑ ⓒ ⓓ	9.	ⓐ ⓑ ⓒ ⓓ	13.	ⓐ ⓑ ⓒ ⓓ	17.	ⓐ ⓑ ⓒ ⓓ
2.	ⓐ ⓑ ⓒ ⓓ	6.	ⓐ ⓑ ⓒ ⓓ	10.	ⓐ ⓑ ⓒ ⓓ	14.	ⓐ ⓑ ⓒ ⓓ	18.	ⓐ ⓑ ⓒ ⓓ
3.	ⓐ ⓑ ⓒ ⓓ	7.	ⓐ ⓑ ⓒ ⓓ	11.	ⓐ ⓑ ⓒ ⓓ	15.	ⓐ ⓑ ⓒ ⓓ	19.	ⓐ ⓑ ⓒ ⓓ
4.	ⓐ ⓑ ⓒ ⓓ	8.	ⓐ ⓑ ⓒ ⓓ	12.	ⓐ ⓑ ⓒ ⓓ	16.	ⓐ ⓑ ⓒ ⓓ	20.	ⓐ ⓑ ⓒ ⓓ

Chapter 04

Early Kingdoms, Republics and Ideas

MCQs 1 Mark Questions

1. In ...., a horse was left to wander for a year. Anyone could challenge the authority of the king by fighting with the warriors who travelled with the horse.

(a) Ashvamedha Yagya (b) Rajsuya Yagya
(c) Soma Yagya (d) None of these

2. Which of the following was/were the main occupation that vaishyas perform?

(a) Farming (b) Waging Wars
(c) Both (a) and (b) (d) Teaching

3. The remains of the earliest Janapadas have been found in India in which of the following places?

(a) Purana Qila, Delhi
(b) Hastinapur, Meerut
(c) Atranjikhera, Etah
(d) All of the above

4. What was the capital of Vajji Janapada?

(a) Shravasti (b) Rajgir
(c) Vaishali (d) Kaushambi

5. Identify the spiritual leaders who belonged to Licchavis clan of Vajji Janapada.

(a) Gautam Buddha
(b) Mahavira Tirthankara
(c) Guru Gobind Singh
(d) Shankaracharya

6. Which of the following crops was/were not prominently grown in the period of Mahajanapadas?

(a) Sesame (b) Mustard
(c) Sugarcane (d) All of these

7. Who among the following was/were the most powerful rulers of Magadha?

(a) Ajatashatru
(b) Bimbisara
(c) Mahapadma Nanda
(d) Both (a) and (b)

8. The first capital of Magadha was Rajgir which was later shifted to ......

(a) Vaishali
(b) Pataliputra
(c) Kushinagar
(d) Shravasti

9. Complete the given analogy.

Brahmins : Study and Teach : :

Kshatriyas : ?

(a) Farming (b) Fighting Battles
(c) Teaching (d) Untouchables

10. Which spiritual leader in Indian belonged to Sakya gana?

(a) Lord Mahavira
(b) Lord Buddha
(c) Rishi Vishwamitra
(d) None of the above

11. In which modern state of India, Buddha attained enlightenment?
(a) Uttar Pradesh (b) Madhya Pradesh
(c) Bihar (d) Haryana

12. The below image is one of the most important Buddhist pilgrimage site. This was a place where Buddha taught his first sermon. Identify the place and find out in which state of India it lies.

(a) Kushinagar, Bihar
(b) Lumbini, Nepal
(c) Sarnath, Uttar Pradesh
(d) Amravati, Andhra Pradesh

13. Complete the given analogy.
Vaishesika : Konada : : ? : Gautama
(a) Nyaya (b) Samkhya
(c) Yoga (d) Purva Mimansa

14. Who amongst the following is credited for preparing grammar for Sanskrit?
(a) Panini (b) Shankaracharya
(c) Patanjali (d) Gotama

15. Which of the following languages was used by Mahavira Tirthankara to preach his ideas?
(a) Sanskrit (b) Pali (c) Prakrit (d) Hindi

16. What principles does the Jainas, followers of Lord Mahavira had to follow?
(a) Observe celibacy
(b) Follow honesty
(c) Abstain from stealing
(d) All of the above

17. In which of the following places, the teachings of Lord Mahavira were written down?
(a) Pataliputra (b) Rajgir
(c) Valabhi (d) Vaishali

18. Vinayapitaka, a rule book for a Sangha is related to which of the following faiths?
(a) Buddhism (b) Jainism
(c) Hinduism (d) Sikhism

19. Karle caves are found in which state?
(a) Odisha (b) Kàrnataka
(c) Maharashtra (d) Tamil Nadu

20. When a person gives up everything he becomes a ....
(a) Samnyasins (b) Grihastha
(c) Vanaprastha (d) Brahmacharya

MCQs 2 Marks Questions

Directions (Q. 21-22) Look at the map given below and answer the following questions.

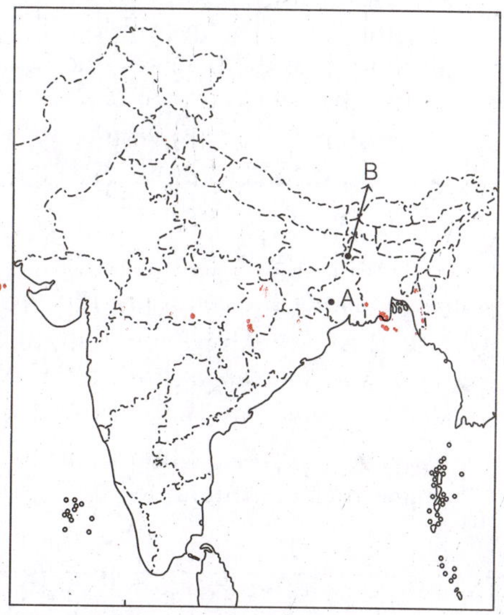

21. Which of the following Mahajanapadas is marked with 'A' in the above map?
(a) Magadha (b) Kaushambi
(c) Kuru (d) Vall

22. Which of the following Mahajanapadas is marked with 'B' in the above map?

(a) Magadha (b) Vajji
(c) Kuru (d) Panchala

23. Consider the following statements regarding agriculture during the period of Mahajanapadas.

I. There was growth in the use of iron plough shares.
II. There was growth in the transplantation of wheat.
III. Transplantation of crop led to the increased production.

Choose the incorrect statements from the options given below.

(a) I and II (b) Only II
(c) I and III (d) I, II and III

24. Read the passage and answer the following question.

More than 2300 years ago, a ruler named 'X', who lived in Macedonia in Europe, wanted to become a world conqueror. He conquered parts of Egypt and West Asia, and came to the Indian sub-continent, reaching up to the banks of the Beas. Identify the personality of X.

(a) Alexander (b) Porus
(c) Seleucus Nicator (d) Vasco da Gama

25. There are two statements marked as Assertion (A) and Reason (R). Mark your answer as per the codes given below.

Assertion (A) All people from different Varna systems were allowed to join the Buddhist Sangha.

Reason (R) Those who joined the Sangha included Brahmins, Kshatriyas and slaves, labourers and barbers.

Codes

(a) Both A and R are true and R is the correct explanation of A
(b) Both A and R are true, but R is not the correct explanation of A
(c) A is true, but R is false
(d) A is false, but R is true

26. Match the following.

List I (School of Philosophy)	List II (Founder)
A. Yoga	1. Kapila
B. Samkhya	2. Patanjali
C. Vedanta	3. Jaimani
D. Poorva Mimansa	4. Vyasa

Codes

	A	B	C	D		A	B	C	D
(a)	1	2	3	4	(b)	4	2	3	1
(c)	3	1	4	2	(d)	2	1	4	3

27. Read the given statements and identifies which ones are true (T) and which ones are false (F).

I. Jains believed in the existence of 30 Tirthankaras.
II. Rishabhdeva was the first Tirthankaras and Mahavira was the last.
III. Lord Mahavira was born in Vajji Janapada.

	I	II	III		I	II	III
(a)	T	T	T	(b)	F	T	F
(c)	F	T	T	(d)	T	F	F

Darken your choice with HB Pencil

1.	ⓐ ⓑ ⓒ ⓓ	6.	ⓐ ⓑ ⓒ ⓓ	11.	ⓐ ⓑ ⓒ ⓓ	16.	ⓐ ⓑ ⓒ ⓓ	21.	ⓐ ⓑ ⓒ ⓓ	26.	ⓐ ⓑ ⓒ ⓓ
2.	ⓐ ⓑ ⓒ ⓓ	7.	ⓐ ⓑ ⓒ ⓓ	12.	ⓐ ⓑ ⓒ ⓓ	17.	ⓐ ⓑ ⓒ ⓓ	22.	ⓐ ⓑ ⓒ ⓓ	27.	ⓐ ⓑ ⓒ ⓓ
3.	ⓐ ⓑ ⓒ ⓓ	8.	ⓐ ⓑ ⓒ ⓓ	13.	ⓐ ⓑ ⓒ ⓓ	18.	ⓐ ⓑ ⓒ ⓓ	23.	ⓐ ⓑ ⓒ ⓓ		
4.	ⓐ ⓑ ⓒ ⓓ	9.	ⓐ ⓑ ⓒ ⓓ	14.	ⓐ ⓑ ⓒ ⓓ	19.	ⓐ ⓑ ⓒ ⓓ	24.	ⓐ ⓑ ⓒ ⓓ		
5.	ⓐ ⓑ ⓒ ⓓ	10.	ⓐ ⓑ ⓒ ⓓ	15.	ⓐ ⓑ ⓒ ⓓ	20.	ⓐ ⓑ ⓒ ⓓ	25.	ⓐ ⓑ ⓒ ⓓ		

Chapter

05

The First Empire : The Mauryas

MCQs 1 Mark Questions

1. ...... was founded by Chandragupta more than 2300 years ago. This dynasty had three important rulers that are Chandragupta, Bindusara and Ashoka.

(a) Gupta dynasty
(b) Maurya dynasty
(c) Mughal dynasty
(d) Ashoka dynasty

2. What are the two provincial capitals of Mauryan Empire?

(a) Jammu and Kandahar
(b) Taxila and Ujjain
(c) Madurai and Sanchi
(d) Kalinga and Kanpur

3. Who sent the Greek ambassador Megasthenes to Chandragupta's Court?

(a) Porus
(b) Seleucus Nicator
(c) Alexander
(d) Darius

4. Chandragupta Maurya established the Maurya Empire with the help of Chanakya who wrote a famous book ....

(a) Dhamma
(b) Devichandraguptam
(c) Arthashastra
(d) Bible

5. Identify the picture with the help of information given below.
This finely polished stone sculpture was part of a Mauryan pillar. Currently, it is placed in Rashtrapati Bhavan.

(a) Pataliputra bull (b) Rampurva bull
(c) Kamdhenu bull (d) Ashoka bull

6. Which of these cities was the gateway to the North-West and Central-Asia?

(a) Pataliputra (b) Kalinga
(c) Taxila (d) Sarnath

7. Choose the odd one out.

(a) Vikramaditya (b) Ashoka
(c) Bindusara (d) Chandragupta

8. Which of the following was/were the feature(s) of the city of Pataliputra (modern Patna)?

(a) It was a large and beautiful city.
(b) It has 500 towers and 64 gates.
(c) The houses of two and three storey were built of wood and mud brick.
(d) Both (a) and (c)

9. What was the meaning of Ashoka's Dhamma?
(a) A set of ideals of social behaviour
(b) A new religion
(c) The court order
(d) Art and craft of Mauryas

10. To which countries did Ashoka send emissaries to spread the ideas of Dhamma?
(a) Syria, Egypt
(b) Greece and Sri Lanka
(c) Both (a) and (b)
(d) United Arab Emirates

11. Most of the inscriptions of Ashoka are written in which of the following language?
(a) Sanskrit
(b) Ancient Greek
(c) Hebrew
(d) Prakrit

12. What amongst the following was not Ashoka's message to his subjects?
(a) One should be harsh with slaves and servants.
(b) Treating all elders with compassion.
(c) Giving gifts to Brahmins and Monks.
(d) Each one should respect the other's religion.

13. Complete the given analogy.
Lion Capital : Delhi : : Ashoka Inscription : ?
(a) Pataliputra (b) Maski
(c) Patna (d) Lucknow

14. Most modern Indian scripts have developed from the .... script.
(a) Indus
(b) Kharosthi
(c) Brahmi
(d) Cuneiform

MCQs 2 Marks Questions

15. Read the given statements and choose which ones are true (T) and which ones are false (F).
I. Bindusara was the grandfather of Chandragupta Maurya.
II. Ujjain lay on the route from North to South.
III. The Lion Capital is taken from stone pillar of Sarnath.

Codes

	I	II	III		I	II	III
(a)	F	F	F	(b)	F	T	F
(c)	F	F	T	(d)	T	F	T

16. Identify the correct statement from the following statements.
(a) Mithila was the ancient name of Orissa.
(b) Chandragupta's ideas were written down in the Arthashastra.
(c) Seleucus Nicator was the emperor of India in 237 BC.
(d) None of the above

17. There are two statements marked as Assertion (A) and Reason (R). Mark your answer as per the codes given below.
Assertion (A) Ashoka was so horrified to see the bloodshed and violence that he decided not to fight any more wars after Kalinga.
Reason (R) Ashoka was the only king in the history who gave up conquest after winning a war.

Codes
(a) Both A and R are true and R is the correct explanation of A
(b) Both A and R are true, but R is not the correct explanation of A
(c) A is true, but R is false
(d) R is true, but A is false

18. On the given map of India, identify the places marked as A and B where the inscriptions of Ashoka were found.

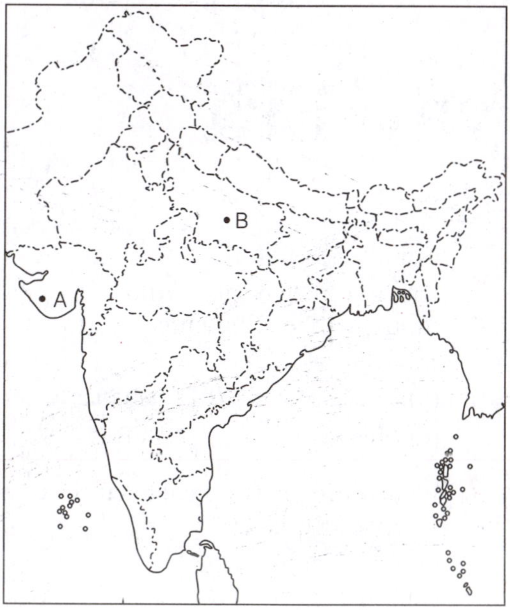

	A	B
(a)	Junagarh	Patna
(b)	Girnar	Allahabad
(c)	Gir	Matsya
(d)	Nashik	Lucknow

19. Consider the following statements with reference to Ashoka's Dhamma.

I. Dhamma is the Prakrit word derived from the Sanskrit word 'Dharma'.

II. Ashoka's Dhamma did not involve worship of a God or performance of a sacrifice.

III. Ashoka appointed Dhamma Mahamattas to punish people who deviated from Dhamma.

Choose the correct statement(s) from the codes given below.

(a) I and II
(b) I and III
(c) Only II
(d) Only III

Darken your choice with HB Pencil

1.	ⓐ ⓑ ⓒ ⓓ	5.	ⓐ ⓑ ⓒ ⓓ	9.	ⓐ ⓑ ⓒ ⓓ	13.	ⓐ ⓑ ⓒ ⓓ	17.	ⓐ ⓑ ⓒ ⓓ
2.	ⓐ ⓑ ⓒ ⓓ	6.	ⓐ ⓑ ⓒ ⓓ	10.	ⓐ ⓑ ⓒ ⓓ	14.	ⓐ ⓑ ⓒ ⓓ	18.	ⓐ ⓑ ⓒ ⓓ
3.	ⓐ ⓑ ⓒ ⓓ	7.	ⓐ ⓑ ⓒ ⓓ	11.	ⓐ ⓑ ⓒ ⓓ	15.	ⓐ ⓑ ⓒ ⓓ	19.	ⓐ ⓑ ⓒ ⓓ
4.	ⓐ ⓑ ⓒ ⓓ	8.	ⓐ ⓑ ⓒ ⓓ	12.	ⓐ ⓑ ⓒ ⓓ	16.	ⓐ ⓑ ⓒ ⓓ		

Chapter
06

Post-Mauryan Era

MCQs 1 Mark Questions

1. Which word was used in Sangam poems for the chiefs of three ruling families of South India?
(a) Muvendar (b) Alexander
(c) Aryavarta (d) Maharaja

2. Identify the dynasties which were ruling major parts of South India around 2300 years ago.
(a) Chera, Chola and Pandya
(b) Chalukya, Chera and Ganga
(c) Satavahana, Kushana and Pandya
(d) Saka, Pratihars and Indo-Greeks

3. Who was the mother of Satavahana ruler, Gautamiputra Shri Satakarni ?
(a) Gautami Laxmi (b) Gautami Kaveri
(c) Gautami Balashri (d) Gautami Shridevi

4. Which item of South India was known as Black Gold in Roman Empire?
(a) Coal (b) Pepper
(c) Ivory (d) Cardamom

5. Identify the path that was followed by the people from China during the ancient times.
(a) Silk Route
(b) Dakshinapatha
(c) Buddhist Dharma Marg
(d) None of the above

6. The best-known rulers who controlled the Silk Route were the ....
(a) Cholas (b) Kushanas
(c) Cheras (d) Pandyas

7. What were the two major centres of power of Kushanas?
(a) Agra and Mathura
(b) Lahore and Kabul
(c) Peshawar and Mathura
(d) Delhi and Kannauj

8. Kushanas were amongst the earliest rulers to issue coins made of ....
(a) gold (b) copper
(c) silver (d) bronze

9. What was the main reason of conflict between the Chalukyas and Pallavas?
(a) Control over the Gangetic Plains
(b) Religious policy of Pallava rulers
(c) Aggressive nature of Chalukyas
(d) Control over the Deccan Plateau regions

10. By which symbol the attainment of enlightenment of Buddha was shown in Buddhist texts?
(a) Horse (b) Flowing water
(c) Peepal tree (d) Lotus

11. The older form of Buddhism is known as ....

(a) Vajrayana (b) Theravada
(c) Gelugpa (d) Mahayana

12. Which form of Buddhism supported the statue building and the concept of Bodhisattvas?

(a) Theravada (b) Vajrayana
(c) Hinayana (d) Mahayana

13. What was the main motive behind the journey of 'Fa Xian, Xuan Zang and I-Qing' to India?

(a) They came to visit places associated with Buddha.
(b) To see the political structure of India.
(c) They came to gather information about Indian rulcrs.
(d) They were forced out of China by the King.

14. Name the sacred book of Hindus that talks about 'Bhakti'.

(a) Ramayana (b) Purana
(c) Panchatantra (d) Bhagavad Gita

15. The word 'Hindu' is derived from which of the following river?

(a) Ganga (b) Yamuna
(c) Indus (d) Saraswati

16. Which form of Buddhism was more popular in South-East Asia, Sri Lanka, Myanmar and Thailand?

(a) Theravada (b) Mahayana
(c) Hinayana (d) Vajrayana

17. The ...... people were the first to produce silk as early as 7000 BCE.

(a) Chinese (b) Persian
(c) British (d) India

18. The Christians of this state or city, known as Syrian Christians, are amongst the oldest Christian communities of the world. Identify the state or city.

(a) Bethlehem (b) Sikkim
(c) Kerala (d) Tamil Nadu

19. On the basis of information given below, identify the image.

This magnificent statue is from Iran, Madhya Pradesh. According to the Puranas, Lord Vishnu took the form of a boar to rescue the Earth, which had sunk into water.

(a) Matsya
(b) Narsimha
(c) Varaha
(d) Nataraja

MCQs 2 Marks Questions

20. Choose the incorrect statement with respect to the Chiefs of Cholas, Cheras and Pandyas.

(a) The Chiefs of these ruling families did not collect regular taxes.
(b) The Chiefs also went on military expeditions and collected tribute from neighbouring areas.
(c) They kept some of the wealth and distributed the rest amongst their supporters.
(d) None of the above

21. With reference to Buddhism, consider the following statements.

I. Nalanda became the most famous Buddhist University.

II. Mahayana Buddhism spread to Sri Lanka, Burma, Thailand and Indonesia.

Choose the correct statement(s) from the codes given below.

(a) Only I (b) Only II
(c) None of these (d) Both (a) and (b)

22. With reference to the passage given below, identify the famous dynasty of ancient India.

They were known as the Lords of Dakshinapatha as they were ruling in the West often controlling the route to the Southern regions. Gautamiputra Shri Satakarni was the most prominent ruler of this dynasty.

(a) Satavahanas (b) Pallavas
(c) Chalukyas (d) Palas

23. Match the following.

List I (Dynasty)	**List II** (Symbol)
A. Chola	1. Bow and Arrow
B. Pandya	2. Fish
C. Chera	3. Tiger

	A	B	C		A	B	C
(a)	1	2	3	(b)	2	3	1
(c)	3	1	2	(d)	3	2	1

24. Consider the following statements about the Kushana rulers of ancient India.

I. The famous Kushana ruler, Kanishka started the Vikram Samvat in 78 CE.

II. Kushanas issued a number of Gold and Copper coins.

Which of the statements given above is/are correct?

(a) Only I (b) Only II
(c) None of these (d) All of these

25. Read the given statements and select the correct option.

Statement (I) Bhakti comes from a Sanskrit term Bhaj, which means 'to divide or share'.

Statement (II) Those who followed the system of Bhakti emphasise devotion of a god or goddess.

Codes

(a) Both statements I and II are correct
(b) Both statements I and II are incorrect
(c) Statement I is correct, but statement II is incorrect
(d) Statement II is correct, but statement I is incorrect

26. Read the following statements and choose which ones are true (T) and which ones are false (F).

I. Bhakti is a form of worship gradually spread to different parts of the country.

II. Bhakti emphasised on the performance of elaborate sacrifices.

III. Worship of certain deities became a central feature of later Hinduism.

Codes

	I	II	III		I	II	III
(a)	T	T	F	(b)	F	T	F
(c)	T	F	T	(d)	F	F	T

Darken your choice with HB Pencil

1. ⓐ ⓑ ⓒ ⓓ	6. ⓐ ⓑ ⓒ ⓓ	11. ⓐ ⓑ ⓒ ⓓ	16. ⓐ ⓑ ⓒ ⓓ	21. ⓐ ⓑ ⓒ ⓓ	26. ⓐ ⓑ ⓒ ⓓ
2. ⓐ ⓑ ⓒ ⓓ	7. ⓐ ⓑ ⓒ ⓓ	12. ⓐ ⓑ ⓒ ⓓ	17. ⓐ ⓑ ⓒ ⓓ	22. ⓐ ⓑ ⓒ ⓓ	
3. ⓐ ⓑ ⓒ ⓓ	8. ⓐ ⓑ ⓒ ⓓ	13. ⓐ ⓑ ⓒ ⓓ	18. ⓐ ⓑ ⓒ ⓓ	23. ⓐ ⓑ ⓒ ⓓ	
4. ⓐ ⓑ ⓒ ⓓ	9. ⓐ ⓑ ⓒ ⓓ	14. ⓐ ⓑ ⓒ ⓓ	19. ⓐ ⓑ ⓒ ⓓ	24. ⓐ ⓑ ⓒ ⓓ	
5. ⓐ ⓑ ⓒ ⓓ	10. ⓐ ⓑ ⓒ ⓓ	15. ⓐ ⓑ ⓒ ⓓ	20. ⓐ ⓑ ⓒ ⓓ	25. ⓐ ⓑ ⓒ ⓓ	

Chapter 07

Early Villages and Towns

MCQs 1 Mark Questions

1. Where was/were the largest collections of iron tools and weapons were found?
(a) Megalithic Burials (b) Paleolithic Burials
(c) Neolithic Burials (d) Both (a) and (b)

2. Agricultural production increased due to an increased use of .... tools.
(a) ceramic (b) iron
(c) copper (d) bronze

3. How did the 'Dasa Karmakara' earn their living in the ancient India?
(a) By begging
(b) By working in other's fields
(c) By performing art
(d) By fighting in the army

4. The ancient South India is famous as the age of 'Sangam'. What does the term Sangam refer to?
(a) Assembly or a Sabha
(b) Confluence of rivers
(c) Age of war
(d) Architectural meetings

5. Sangam literature, composed around 2300 years ago, were held in which of the following cities?
(a) Varanasi (b) Nalanda
(c) Prayag (d) Madurai

6. Choose the odd one out.
(a) Pataliputra (b) Prayag
(c) Ujjain (d) Madurai

7. Identify the coins in the image given below.

(a) Golden bead
(b) Punch-marked coins
(c) Silver Tanka
(d) Shehanshah

8. Which of the following were the items that were imported into Barygaza (Greek name for Bharuch)?
(a) Copper and wine (b) Ivory and cotton
(c) Silk and coal (d) Perfumes

9. Name the coastal port town that exported textiles, beads, precious stones and imported wine and olive oil from Rome.
(a) Kaveripattinam (b) Puhar
(c) Arikamedu (d) Pataliputra

10. Identify the pottery with the help of picture given below.

(a) Northern Black Polished Ware
(b) Stamped Red-Glazed Pottery
(c) Ceramic Ware
(d) Arretine Ware

11. How did Northern Black Polished Ware (NBPW) got its name?
(a) They were black in colour.
(b) They were found in Northern part.
(c) They were placed North facing.
(d) They were polished with paint.

12. Northern Black Polished Ware was known for its ....
(a) Farmers Association
(b) Fine agricultural tools
(c) Fine Pottery
(d) Finished Ornaments

13. What was the association of merchants called?
(a) Sabha (b) Mandi
(c) Shreni (d) Palika

14. .... were rows of pots of ceramic rings placed one on top of the other. These were probably used as toilets, drains or as garbage bins.
(a) NBPW (b) Punch-marked coins
(c) Ring wells (d) Shrenis

15. Mathura, Varanasi, Prayag and Srirangam were famous for which of the following?
(a) Religious and temple towns
(b) Trading centres
(c) Bead manufacturing units
(d) Capital cities

16. 'Amphorae' were used for which purpose?
(a) To contain liquids
(b) To keep the horses
(c) For lightening lamps
(d) To keep the artillery

17. Choose the incorrectly matched pair.
(a) Grama Bhojaka – Village headman
(b) Uzhavar – Ordinary ploughman
(c) Kadaisiyar – Landless labourer
(d) None of the above

18. Ashtadhyayi, a contemporary book of grammar was written by ....
(a) Kalidas (b) Panini
(c) Vishnugupta (d) Patanjali

19. Who among the following ruled around 2000 years ago and found the Rome city of Europe?
(a) Romulus (b) Numa Pompilius
(c) Hostilius (d) Augustus

20. On the basis of the information given below, identify the image.

These stories narrate the events relating to the Buddha and records his teachings. A stunning representation of these stories are found in a medallion at Bharhut.

(a) Panchatantra (b) Jataka
(c) Arthshastra (d) Ashtadhyayi

MCQs 2 Marks Questions

21. Read the following statements about the punch-marked coins and choose which ones are true (T) or which ones are false (F).

I. These coins were called punch-marked coins because of their colour.

II. These coins were made of silver and copper.

III. These coins were rectangular, square and sometimes round in shape.

Codes

	I	II	III		I	II	III
(a)	F	T	T	(b)	F	T	F
(c)	T	F	T	(d)	T	T	F

22. Consider the following statements about the Grama Bhojakas.

I. Grama Bhojaka had no land of his own.

II. He collects taxes on behalf of the king.

III. He also functioned as the judge and policeman of the village.

Which of the statements given above is/are correct?

(a) Both I and II (b) Both II and III
(c) Both I and III (d) Only III

23. Match the following.

List I (City)	List II (Famous for)
A. Madurai/Varanasi	1. Making beads
B. Uraiyur	2. Dyeing cloth
C. Mathura	3. Making sculptures
D. Arikamedu	4. Manufacturing cloth

Codes

	A	B	C	D
(a)	3	4	2	1
(b)	4	1	2	3
(c)	4	2	3	1
(d)	2	1	4	3

24. Identify the city with regards to the following statements given below.

- It was important because it was located on the crossroads of two major routes of travel and trade from the North-West to the East and from North to South.
- Around 2000 years ago, this city became the second capital of Kushanas.

Codes

(a) Ujjain
(b) Pataliputra
(c) Taxila
(d) Mathura

25. There are two statements marked as Assertion (A) and Reason (R). Mark your answer as per the codes given below.

Assertion (A) Sangam Literature was composed around 2300 years ago.

Reason (R) These texts were supposed to have been composed and compiled in sangams of poets.

Codes

(a) Both A and R are true and R is the correct explanation of A
(b) Both A and R are true, but R is not the correct explanation of A
(c) A is true, but R is false
(d) A is false, but R is true

Darken your choice with HB Pencil

1.	ⓐ ⓑ ⓒ ⓓ	6.	ⓐ ⓑ ⓒ ⓓ	11.	ⓐ ⓑ ⓒ ⓓ	16.	ⓐ ⓑ ⓒ ⓓ	21.	ⓐ ⓑ ⓒ ⓓ
2.	ⓐ ⓑ ⓒ ⓓ	7.	ⓐ ⓑ ⓒ ⓓ	12.	ⓐ ⓑ ⓒ ⓓ	17.	ⓐ ⓑ ⓒ ⓓ	22.	ⓐ ⓑ ⓒ ⓓ
3.	ⓐ ⓑ ⓒ ⓓ	8.	ⓐ ⓑ ⓒ ⓓ	13.	ⓐ ⓑ ⓒ ⓓ	18.	ⓐ ⓑ ⓒ ⓓ	23.	ⓐ ⓑ ⓒ ⓓ
4.	ⓐ ⓑ ⓒ ⓓ	9.	ⓐ ⓑ ⓒ ⓓ	14.	ⓐ ⓑ ⓒ ⓓ	19.	ⓐ ⓑ ⓒ ⓓ	24.	ⓐ ⓑ ⓒ ⓓ
5.	ⓐ ⓑ ⓒ ⓓ	10.	ⓐ ⓑ ⓒ ⓓ	15.	ⓐ ⓑ ⓒ ⓓ	20.	ⓐ ⓑ ⓒ ⓓ	25.	ⓐ ⓑ ⓒ ⓓ

Chapter 08

New Kingdoms and Empires

MCQs 1 Mark Questions

1. What were the inscriptions that were composed in the praise of rulers?
   (a) Kavya Sangati
   (b) Prashasti
   (c) Rajtarangini
   (d) Biography

2. For which ruler, Harisena composed Prayag Prashasti?
   (a) Ashoka
   (b) Skandagupta
   (c) Chandragupta II
   (d) Samudragupta

3. What was the old name of Allahabad?
   (a) Kashi
   (b) Vajji
   (c) Prayag
   (d) Halebid

4. Nine rulers of .... were uprooted and their kingdoms were made a part of Samudragupta's Empire.
   (a) Aryavarta
   (b) Ceylon
   (c) Dakshinapatha
   (d) Sangam

5. Chandragupta II started the Vikram Samvat to commemorate whom among the following?
   (a) Victory over Kushanas
   (b) Victory over Sakas
   (c) His 50th birth anniversary
   (d) Birth anniversary of Buddha

6. Which Gupta king adopted the title of 'Vikramaditya'?
   (a) Srigupta
   (b) Vishnugupta
   (c) Kumaragupta
   (d) Chandragupta II

7. Who among the following married a Lichchhavi princess Kumaradevi to enhance his prestige?
   (a) Samudragupta
   (b) Chandragupta I
   (c) Kumaragupta
   (d) Pulakeshin II

8. Identify the first Gupta ruler to adopt the title of 'Maharajadhiraja'.
   (a) Chandragupta I
   (b) Bindusara
   (c) Samudragupta
   (d) Srigupta

9. Chinese traveller, Xuanzang spent a lot of time in the court of which Indian ruler?
(a) Vikramaditya
(b) Harshavardhana
(c) Chandragupta Maurya
(d) Kanishka

10. Which of the following was/were written by Harshavardhana?
(a) Ratnavali
(b) Priyadarshika
(c) Mahananda
(d) All of the above

11. .... was the author of 'Harshacharita', a biography of Harshavardhana.
(a) Kalidasa
(b) Shudraka
(c) Vishakhadatta
(d) Banabhatta

12. The kingdom of which dynasty was centred around the Raichur Doab, between the rivers Krishna and Tungabhadra?
(a) Pallava (b) Satavahana
(c) Rashtrakuta (d) Chalukya

13. Identify the correctly matched pair.
(a) Harshavardhana – Thanesar
(b) Chalukyas – Kanchipuram
(c) Pallavas – Aihole
(d) None of the above

14. Which Chalukyan ruler stopped Harshavardhana's march into Deccan?
(a) Gautamiputra Satkarni
(b) Kirtivarman I
(c) Pulakeshin II
(d) Mangalesha

15. During whose reign, the Aihole Inscription script was composed?
(a) Pulakeshin II
(b) Chandragupta II
(c) Harshavardhana
(d) Kanishka

16. What was the capital of Pallava dynasty?
(a) Kanchipuram
(b) Madurai
(c) Hampi
(d) Kaveripattinam

17. Choose the odd one out.
(a) Banabhatta
(b) Harisena
(c) Kalidasa
(d) Harshavardhana

18. Which court poet of Samudragupta was given the duty of 'Mahadandanayaka'?
(a) Harisena
(b) Vatsabhatti
(c) Kalidasa
(d) Banabhatta

19. What was the main source of income of Gupta Empire?
(a) War proceeds
(b) Land revenue
(c) Tributes from the kings
(d) Gold export

20. Abhigyan Shakuntalam is the love story of .... and ....
(a) Bharat, Sunaina
(b) Dushyanta, Shakuntala
(c) Arjuna, Subhadra
(d) Harsha, Kumaradevi

MCQs 2 Marks Questions

21. Consider the following Gupta rulers and arrange them in the chronological order.

I. Skandagupta
II. Chandragupta I
III. Chandragupta II
IV. Kumaragupta

Codes

(a) II, III, IV and I
(b) II, III, I and IV
(c) I, II, III and IV
(d) IV, III, II and I

22. Read the following statements and select the correct option.

Statement (I) The Gupta period is known as the 'Golden Age' of Indian history.

Statement (II) Under the Guptas, there was great development in the fields of art, literature and technology.

(a) Both statements I and II are correct
(b) Both statements I and II are incorrect
(c) Statement I is correct, but statement II is incorrect
(d) Statement II is correct, but statement I is incorrect

23. Unscramble the given letters to obtain the name of a capital city.

HELIOA

Select the option that correctly identifies the dynasty of this capital city.

(a) Pallavas (b) Chalukya
(c) Pandyas (d) Cheras

24. Consider the following statements about the administration during the Gupta period.

I. Harisena held three posts of Mahadandanayaka, Kumaramatya and Sandhivigrahika.
II. Military leaders were paid salary in the cash.
III. Sarthavaha were the leaders of merchant caravans.

Which of the statements given above is/are correct?

(a) I and II
(b) II and III
(c) I and III
(d) I, II and III

25. Identify the leaders from the information given below.

- These were military leaders who provided the king with the troops whenever he needed them.
- They were not paid regular salaries. Instead, some of them received grants of lands. Whenever the ruler was weak, they tried to became independent.

(a) Amatyas
(b) Samantas
(c) Ayuktas
(d) Nayakas

26. Match the following.

	List I		List II
A.	Ur	1.	Head of scribes
B.	Sabha	2.	Organisation of merchants
C.	Nagaram	3.	Assembly of Brahmin land owners
D.	Prathama kulika	4.	Assembly of non-brahmins

Codes

	A	B	C	D
(a)	3	4	2	1
(b)	4	1	2	3
(c)	4	2	3	1
(d)	2	1	4	3

27. On the given map of India, identify the places where kingdoms of Aryavarta in the Gupta Era are found.

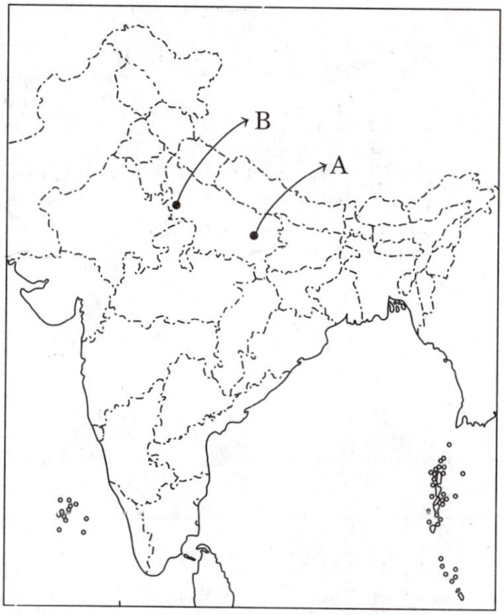

	A	B
(a)	Prayag	Mathura
(b)	Ujjain	Gandhara
(c)	Kannauj	Pataliputra
(d)	Amravati	Mathura

28. Read the following statements and choose which ones are true (T) and which ones are false (F).

I. Ur was a village assembly where land owners were not Brahmins.

II. Nagaram was an organisation of artists.

III. Assemblies were controlled by Brahmins.

Codes

	I	II	III
(a)	F	T	T
(b)	F	F	T
(c)	T	T	T
(d)	T	F	F

Darken your choice with HB Pencil

1.	ⓐ ⓑ ⓒ ⓓ	6.	ⓐ ⓑ ⓒ ⓓ	11.	ⓐ ⓑ ⓒ ⓓ	16.	ⓐ ⓑ ⓒ ⓓ	21.	ⓐ ⓑ ⓒ ⓓ	26.	ⓐ ⓑ ⓒ ⓓ
2.	ⓐ ⓑ ⓒ ⓓ	7.	ⓐ ⓑ ⓒ ⓓ	12.	ⓐ ⓑ ⓒ ⓓ	17.	ⓐ ⓑ ⓒ ⓓ	22.	ⓐ ⓑ ⓒ ⓓ	27.	ⓐ ⓑ ⓒ ⓓ
3.	ⓐ ⓑ ⓒ ⓓ	8.	ⓐ ⓑ ⓒ ⓓ	13.	ⓐ ⓑ ⓒ ⓓ	18.	ⓐ ⓑ ⓒ ⓓ	23.	ⓐ ⓑ ⓒ ⓓ	28.	ⓐ ⓑ ⓒ ⓓ
4.	ⓐ ⓑ ⓒ ⓓ	9.	ⓐ ⓑ ⓒ ⓓ	14.	ⓐ ⓑ ⓒ ⓓ	19.	ⓐ ⓑ ⓒ ⓓ	24.	ⓐ ⓑ ⓒ ⓓ		
5.	ⓐ ⓑ ⓒ ⓓ	10.	ⓐ ⓑ ⓒ ⓓ	15.	ⓐ ⓑ ⓒ ⓓ	20.	ⓐ ⓑ ⓒ ⓓ	25.	ⓐ ⓑ ⓒ ⓓ		

Chapter

09

Art, Culture and Science

MCQs 1 Mark Questions

1. Harappans manufactured bronze by mixing ....
   (a) copper and iron
   (b) copper and tin
   (c) iron and gold
   (d) silver and iron

2. Who built the Iron Pillar at Mehrauli, Delhi in his reign?
   (a) Samudragupta
   (b) Ramagupta
   (c) Chandragupta II
   (d) Skandagupta

3. What is the meaning of word 'Stupa'?
   (a) Mound (b) Temple
   (c) Chariot (d) Done

4. Stupas contain the bodily remains (such as teeth, bones or ashes) of which of the following?
   (a) Emperor Ashoka
   (b) Chandragupta II
   (c) Buddha or his followers
   (d) Mahavira

5. A box which is an important part of stupa is known as ....
   (a) relic casket (b) bodily casket
   (c) bone casket (d) None of these

6. Identify the picture with the information given below.

Today this pillar stands in the Qutub Complex that locates in Mehrauli, Delhi.
   (a) Iron Pillar
   (b) Prayag Prashasti
   (c) Junagarh Inscription
   (d) Basilica of Bom

7. A tower built on the top of the Garbhagriha of temples, is known as ....
   (a) Mandapa (b) Shikhara
   (c) Vimana (d) Pradakshina path

8. In which part of temples, the image of chief deity was placed?
   (a) Garbhagriha (b) Gopuram
   (c) Mandapa (d) Shikhara

9. Hastinapur was the capital of which dynasty of ancient India?
(a) Mauryas (b) Palas
(c) Kurus (d) Chandelas

10. What was the capital of Kosala, which is an ancient kingdom and one of the sixteen Mahajanapadas?
(a) Mathura (b) Prayag
(c) Kashi (d) Ayodhya

11. Which of the following contain stories about gods and goddesses such as Vishnu, Shiva, Durga or Parvati?
(a) Puranas (b) Jatakas
(c) Vedas (d) Bhagvad Gita

12. Choose the odd one out.
(a) Ajanta
(b) Ellora
(c) Mahabalipuram
(d) Elephanta

13. Identify the caves in the image given below with the help of the following information.

These caves were built between the 2nd century BCE and the 8th century BCE. Situated near Aurangabad, they are well-known for their cave architecture, sculptures and murals.

(a) Elephanta Caves
(b) Mahabalipuram Caves
(c) Ajanta Caves
(d) Barbar Caves

14. Durga temple, built around 1400 years ago is situated at ....
(a) Kanpur (b) Mandsaur
(c) Aihole (d) Vatapi

15. What is/are the theme of the epic Mahabharata?
(a) Struggle for property in joint family
(b) War between Kaurava and Pandavas
(c) Both (a) and (b)
(d) None of the above

16. What is the theme of 'Aryabhattiyam' a book written by Aryabhatta?
(a) Medicine (b) Astrology
(c) Astronomy (d) Architecture

17. Charaka and Sushruta were famous proponents of ....
(a) Ayurveda (b) Mathematics
(c) Metallurgy (d) Physics

18. Which of the following books deals with surgical procedure?
(a) Charaka Samhita
(b) Susruta Samhita
(c) Aryabhatiyam
(d) None of the above

MCQs 2 Marks Questions

19. Match the following.

List I	List II
A. Ramayana	1. Vyasa
B. Sushruta Samhita	2. Kalidasa
C. Mahabharata	3. Valmiki
D. Raghuvamsa	4. Sushruta

Codes

	A	B	C	D		A	B	C	D
(a)	3	4	1	2	(b)	4	1	2	3
(c)	3	1	4	2	(d)	2	1	4	3

20. Fill in the blanks with appropriate words.

......(A)...... was composed by ......(B)...... in which a monsoon cloud is imagined to be messenger between lovers who are separated from one another.

	A	B
(a)	Abhigyan Shakuntalam	Shudraka
(b)	Manimekalai	Sattanar
(c)	Thirukural	Thiruvalluvar
(d)	Meghduta	Kalidasa

21. Read the following statements and choose which ones are true (T) and which ones are false (F).

I. Puranas literally mean of ancient times.

II. Panchatantra was written by Vishnu Sharma during the Gupta period.

III. Jatakas tells us about the previous lives of the Buddha.

	I	II	III		I	II	III
(a)	F	F	T	(b)	F	T	T
(c)	T	T	F	(d)	T	T	T

22. Consider the following statements about the Puranas.

I. Puranas means religious moral story.

II. Puranas were created in simple Sanskrit language.

III. Women and Shudras were not allowed to hear the recital of Puranas.

Which of the statements given above is/are correct?

(a) Only I (b) Only II

(c) II and III (d) All of these

23. Identify the famous personality on the basis of information given below.

- He was mathematician and astronomer.
- He stated that day and night were caused by the rotation of the Earth on its axis.
- He found a way of calculating the circumference of a circle and developed a scientific explanation for eclipses as well.

(a) Varahamihira

(b) Kanad

(c) Aryabhatta

(d) Bhashkaracharya

24. There are two statements marked as Assertion (A) and Reason (R). Mark your answer as per the codes given below.

Assertion (A) The great Stupa of Sanchi is known as worldwide for its sophisticated architecture.

Reason (R) The brick mound of the Great Stupa at Sanchi dates back to the time of Ashoka while the railings and gateways were added during the time of later rulers.

Codes

(a) Both A and R are true and R is the correct explanation of A

(b) Both A and R are true, but R is not the correct explanation of A

(c) A is true, but R is false

(d) A is false, but R is true

Darken your choice with HB Pencil

1.	ⓐ ⓑ ⓒ ⓓ	5.	ⓐ ⓑ ⓒ ⓓ	9.	ⓐ ⓑ ⓒ ⓓ	13.	ⓐ ⓑ ⓒ ⓓ	17.	ⓐ ⓑ ⓒ ⓓ	21.	ⓐ ⓑ ⓒ ⓓ
2.	ⓐ ⓑ ⓒ ⓓ	6.	ⓐ ⓑ ⓒ ⓓ	10.	ⓐ ⓑ ⓒ ⓓ	14.	ⓐ ⓑ ⓒ ⓓ	18.	ⓐ ⓑ ⓒ ⓓ	22.	ⓐ ⓑ ⓒ ⓓ
3.	ⓐ ⓑ ⓒ ⓓ	7.	ⓐ ⓑ ⓒ ⓓ	11.	ⓐ ⓑ ⓒ ⓓ	15.	ⓐ ⓑ ⓒ ⓓ	19.	ⓐ ⓑ ⓒ ⓓ	23.	ⓐ ⓑ ⓒ ⓓ
4.	ⓐ ⓑ ⓒ ⓓ	8.	ⓐ ⓑ ⓒ ⓓ	12.	ⓐ ⓑ ⓒ ⓓ	16.	ⓐ ⓑ ⓒ ⓓ	20.	ⓐ ⓑ ⓒ ⓓ	24.	ⓐ ⓑ ⓒ ⓓ

Chapter 10

Earth and the Solar System

MCQs 1 Mark Questions

1. Saptarishi forms a part of .... constellation.
(a) Ursa Major (b) Ursa Minor
(c) Scorpion (d) Alpha

2. What is the literal meaning of Greek word Planetai?
(a) Planets (b) Earth
(c) Wanderers (d) Explorers

3. Which among the following planets is considered as 'Earth's twin' due to its similar shape and size?
(a) Mercury (b) Venus
(c) Mars (d) Jupiter

4. The shape of the Earth is taken to be spherical which is not correct. What is the correct shape of the Earth?
(a) Elliptical
(b) Geoid
(c) Ball-shaped
(d) None of the above

5. The distance that light covers in a year by travelling at a speed of 300,000 kms per second is called ....
(a) Cosmic distance
(b) Light year
(c) Orbit
(d) Annual distance

6. Identify the object shown in the picture given below.

(a) Comet (b) Nebulae (c) Star (d) Asteroid

7. The word satellite is derived from the Latin word Satelles which means ....
(a) artificial (b) moon-like
(c) attendant (d) communicator

8. Choose the incorrectly matched pair.
(a) Natural Satellite — Phobos
(b) Constellations — Ursa Major
(c) Galaxy — Andromeda
(d) Earth — Meteoroid

9. Which of the following are classified as 'Dwarf Planets'?
(a) Eris and Uranus (b) Ceres and Uranus
(c) Eris and Ceres (d) Pluto and Uranus

10. Rings around Jupiter, Saturn and Uranus are made up of ice, rocks and ....
(a) gases
(b) small debris
(c) asteroids and meteoroids
(d) satellite debris

11. Identify the incorrect statement about stars.
(a) They are made up of hot and burning gases.
(b) They are huge in size.
(c) They are smaller in size.
(d) They move around the centre of galaxy.

12. Asteroids are found between the orbits of .... and ....
(a) Mars, Jupiter (b) Mercury, Venus
(c) Jupiter, Saturn (d) Saturn, Uranus

13. In ancient times, when there was no easy access to a watch or a compass, travellers would often find their way with the help of the North Star. Which of the following was indicated by the North Star?
(a) North direction
(b) North direction with respect to viewer's position.
(c) Sun's position when it faces North.
(d) Moon's position when it's in North.

14. Which of the following statements is/are correct with respect to Sun?
(a) Sun is the largest object of the Solar System.
(b) The Sun is about 150 million km away from Earth.
(c) Both (a) and (b)
(d) None of the above

15. What are the people known as who study the Celestial Bodies?
(a) Astrologers (b) Astronomers
(c) Physicist (d) Meteorologist

16. Who is considered to be the father of modern astronomy?
(a) Galileo
(b) Copernicus
(c) Johannes Kepler
(d) Edmund Halley

17. How much time is taken by the Moon to complete one revolution around the Earth?
(a) 21 days (b) 23 days
(c) 25 days (d) 27 days

18. Which of the following statements is incorrect regarding to the Moon?
(a) Moon's diameter is only one-quarter that of the Earth.
(b) Moon is about 3,84,400 km away from us.
(c) Only one side of the Moon is visible to us on the Earth.
(d) Moon has conditions favourable for life.

19. Neil Armstrong and two of his partners landed on the Moon on 21st July, 1969. Who among the following were the two partners of Neil Armstrong?
(a) Alan Bean and Michael Collins
(b) Michael Collins and Yuri Gagrin
(c) Edwin Aldrin and Michael Collins
(d) Edwin Aldrin and Alan Bean

MCQs 2 Marks Questions

20. Fill in the blanks with appropriate words. Mercury, Venus, Earth and Mars are known as ......(A)...... while Jupiter, Saturn, Uranus and Neptune are known as ......(B)...... .

	A	B
(a)	Terrestrial planets	Gas Giants
(b)	Gas Giants	Terrestrial Planets
(c)	Celestial bodies	Gas Giants
(d)	Constellations	Celestial bodies

21. Read the following statements and select which ones are true (T) and which ones are false (F).
I. The planets grow in size as they move farther away from the Sun.
II. All the planets of the Solar System move around the Sun on fixed paths.

III. The path on which Solar system move around the Moon is called orbits.

Codes

	I	II	III
(a)	T	T	F
(b)	F	T	F
(c)	F	F	T
(d)	F	F	F

22. Fill in the blanks with appropriate words. The universe is made up of numerous bodies and phenomenon which are at times visible to the naked eye. These objects which are in the sky are known as ......(A)...... . One such body......(B)...... . There are millions of such galaxies which make the universe.

	A	B
(a)	Celestial Bodies	Galaxy
(b)	Galaxy	Constellation
(c)	Celestial Bodies	Nebulae
(d)	Solar System	Constellation

23. There are two statements marked as Assertion (A) and Reason (R). Mark your answer as per the codes given below.

Assertion (A) Small pieces of rock which move around the Sun are called meteoroids.

Reason (R) Sometimes a meteor without being completely burnt falls on the Earth and creates a hollow.

Codes

(a) Both A and R are true and R is the correct explanation of A

(b) Both A and R are true, but R is not the correct explanation of A

(c) A is true, but R is false

(d) A is false, but R is true

24. Match the following.

List I (Planets)	List II (No. of Moons)
A. Mars	1. 1
B. Jupiter	2. 27
C. Uranus	3. 2
D. Earth	4. 53

Codes

	A	B	C	D
(a)	1	2	3	4
(b)	3	4	2	1
(c)	4	3	2	1
(d)	1	2	4	3

25. Consider the following statements.

I. The Solar System is a part of the Milky Way Galaxy.

II. A Galaxy is a huge system of billions of Stars, clouds of dust and gases.

Which of the above statements is/are correct?

(a) Only I (b) Only II

(c) Both I and II (d) None of these

Darken your choice with HB Pencil

1.	ⓐ ⓑ ⓒ ⓓ	6.	ⓐ ⓑ ⓒ ⓓ	11.	ⓐ ⓑ ⓒ ⓓ	16.	ⓐ ⓑ ⓒ ⓓ	21.	ⓐ ⓑ ⓒ ⓓ
2.	ⓐ ⓑ ⓒ ⓓ	7.	ⓐ ⓑ ⓒ ⓓ	12.	ⓐ ⓑ ⓒ ⓓ	17.	ⓐ ⓑ ⓒ ⓓ	22.	ⓐ ⓑ ⓒ ⓓ
3.	ⓐ ⓑ ⓒ ⓓ	8.	ⓐ ⓑ ⓒ ⓓ	13.	ⓐ ⓑ ⓒ ⓓ	18.	ⓐ ⓑ ⓒ ⓓ	23.	ⓐ ⓑ ⓒ ⓓ
4.	ⓐ ⓑ ⓒ ⓓ	9.	ⓐ ⓑ ⓒ ⓓ	14.	ⓐ ⓑ ⓒ ⓓ	19.	ⓐ ⓑ ⓒ ⓓ	24.	ⓐ ⓑ ⓒ ⓓ
5.	ⓐ ⓑ ⓒ ⓓ	10.	ⓐ ⓑ ⓒ ⓓ	15.	ⓐ ⓑ ⓒ ⓓ	20.	ⓐ ⓑ ⓒ ⓓ	25.	ⓐ ⓑ ⓒ ⓓ

Chapter 11

Globe and Motions of the Earth

MCQs 1 Mark Questions

1. Which of the following is a true model (miniature form) of the Earth?
(a) Map
(b) Globe
(c) Sketch
(d) Semantic Map

2. A needle is fixed through the Globe in a tilted manner, which is called ....
(a) orbital plane
(b) longitude
(c) latitude
(d) axis

3. Which among the following is a very important reference point to locate places on the Earth?
(a) Equator
(b) Orbital plane
(c) Longitude
(d) Latitude

4. Identify the incorrect feature with regard to the Globe.
(a) It may be of varying size and type.
(b) It shows countries, continents and oceans in their correct size.
(c) Its period of rotation is known as earthday.
(d) It has a two-dimensional presentation.

5. Complete the given analogy.
Prime Meridian : Longitude :: ? : Latitude
(a) International Date Line
(b) Equator
(c) North Pole
(d) South Pole

6. Choose the odd one out.
(a) Earth (b) Orbit
(c) Latitude (d) Meridian

7. Which of the following statements is incorrect about Prime Meridian?
(a) Its value is 60°.
(b) It divides the Earth into two equal halves.
(c) It passes through Greenwich, where the British Royal Observatory is located.
(d) The Prime Meridian is 0° longitude.

8. Identify the phenomena which is/are depicted in the image given below.

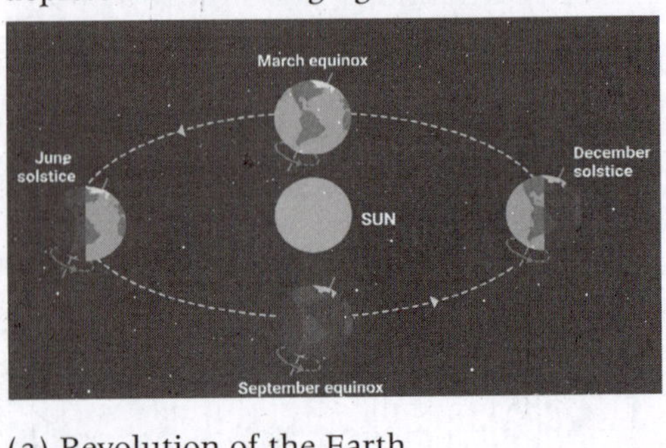

(a) Revolution of the Earth
(b) Changing Seasons
(c) Both (a) and (b)
(d) Neither (a) nor (b)

9. The zone which lies between the Tropic of Cancer and the Tropic of Capricorn is ....
(a) Temperate Zone
(b) Torrid Zone
(c) Frigid Zone
(d) Tropical Zone

10. Belo Horizonate in Brazil (South America) is located on parallels of about which latitude?
(a) 10° North (b) 20° North
(c) 10° South (d) 20° South

11. Tonga Islands are situated on the 20° South latitude which is found in ...... ocean.
(a) Arctic (b) Atlantic
(c) Pacific (d) Indian

12. Which of the following countries do not come in the Arctic Circle?
(a) Finland
(b) Alaska (USA)
(c) Germany
(d) Norway

13. When does the direct rays of the Sun fall on the equator?
(a) 21st March (b) 23rd September
(c) 21st September (d) Both (a) and (b)

MCQs 2 Marks Questions

14. Fill in the blanks with appropriate words.
The Prime Meridian passes through the ....(A)........ at Greenwich near London. Opposite to Prime meridian is the ....(B)......... longitude which is regarded as the International Date Line.

	A	B
(a)	British Royal Observatory	180°
(b)	Palomar Observatory	0°
(c)	British Royal Observatory	0°
(d)	Palomar Observatory	180°

15. Read the passage and answer the following question.
In 1530, a Polish astronomer first wrote in book that the Earth spins daily on its axis and also wrote that the Earth goes around the Sun once in a every year, together with the other planets of the Solar System. Identify the personality.
(a) Galileo (b) Copernicus
(c) Newton (d) Glogow

16. Refer to the venn diagram and select the option that identifies X.

(a) Summer Solstice (b) Winter Solstice
(c) Autumn Solstice (d) Spring Solstice

17. There are two statements marked as Assertion (A) and Reason (R). Mark your answer as per the codes given below.
Assertion (A) The mid-day Sun never shines overhead on any latitude beyond Tropic of Cancer and Tropic of Capricorn.
Reason (R) The angle of the Sun' goes on increasing towards the po'
Codes
(a) Both A and R are true and R correct explanation of A
(b) Both A and R are true, but R is not the correct explanation of A
(c) A is true, but R is false
(d) A is false, but R is true

18. Consider the following statements.

I. Local time can be reckoned by the shadow cast by the Sun.

II. The shadow of the Sun is longest at noon and shortest at sunrise and sunset.

Which of the above statements is/are incorrect?

(a) Only I (b) Only II

(c) Both I and II (d) None of these

19. Match the following.

List I (Latitudes)	List II (Importance)
A. 66½° N	1. Southern limit of overhead sunrays
B. 23 ½° S	2. Northern limit beyond which there can daylight or darkness for more than 24 hours
C. 23½° N	3. Southern limit beyond which there can daylight or darkness for more than 24 hours
D. 66 ½° S	4. Northern limit of overhead sunrays

Codes

	A	B	C	D
(a)	3	4	1	2
(b)	3	1	2	4
(c)	4	3	2	1
(d)	2	1	4	3

20. Read the following statements about great circles and select which ones are true (T) and which ones are false (F).

I. Each longitude and its corresponding latitude make great circles.

II. Equator is also a great circle.

III. Great circles form the shortest distances between two places on Earth.

	I	II	III
(a)	T	F	F
(b)	F	F	T
(c)	T	F	T
(d)	F	T	T

Darken your choice with HB Pencil

1.	ⓐ ⓑ ⓒ ⓓ	5.	ⓐ ⓑ ⓒ ⓓ	9.	ⓐ ⓑ ⓒ ⓓ	13.	ⓐ ⓑ ⓒ ⓓ	17.	ⓐ ⓑ ⓒ ⓓ
2.	ⓐ ⓑ ⓒ ⓓ	6.	ⓐ ⓑ ⓒ ⓓ	10.	ⓐ ⓑ ⓒ ⓓ	14.	ⓐ ⓑ ⓒ ⓓ	18.	ⓐ ⓑ ⓒ ⓓ
3.	ⓐ ⓑ ⓒ ⓓ	7.	ⓐ ⓑ ⓒ ⓓ	11.	ⓐ ⓑ ⓒ ⓓ	15.	ⓐ ⓑ ⓒ ⓓ	19.	ⓐ ⓑ ⓒ ⓓ
4.	ⓐ ⓑ ⓒ ⓓ	8.	ⓐ ⓑ ⓒ ⓓ	12.	ⓐ ⓑ ⓒ ⓓ	16.	ⓐ ⓑ ⓒ ⓓ	20.	ⓐ ⓑ ⓒ ⓓ

Chapter 12

Maps

MCQs 1 Mark Questions

1. Which of the following is not a feature of a map?
(a) Scale (b) Title
(c) Legend (Symbols) (d) Time

2. What is the ratio between the actual distance on the ground and the distance shown on the map called?
(a) Ground Distance (b) Scale of Map
(c) Legend (d) Assumed Distance

3. Identify the figure below and choose the correct answer from the given options.

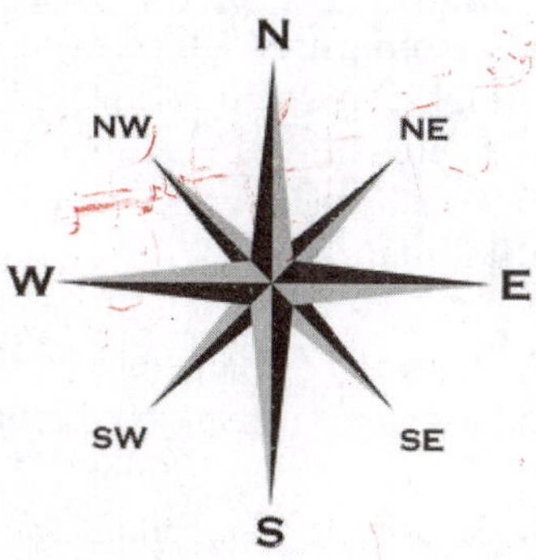

(a) Cardinal Directions
(b) Compass
(c) North Direction
(d) All of the above

4. How many major cardinal directions are there in maps?
(a) 4
(b) 6
(c) 8
(d) 12

5. Which of the following is not a component of map?
(a) Distance
(b) Direction
(c) Relief
(d) Symbol

6. Match the incorrect pair.
(a) Map – Covers a large area
(b) Sketch – Drawn without a scale
(c) Atlas – Not drawn to scale
(d) Plan – Shows accurate detail

7. Choose the correct statement(s) regarding the map.
(a) A map is a detailed drawing of small areas.
(b) A map can show length and breadth of an area.
(c) In a map, there is only one kind of scale to be followed.
(d) All of the above

8. ...... are in use when large areas like continents or countries are to be shown on a paper.
(a) Thematic Maps
(b) Relief Maps
(c) Small Scale Maps
(d) Large Scale Maps

9. What does the given picture portray?

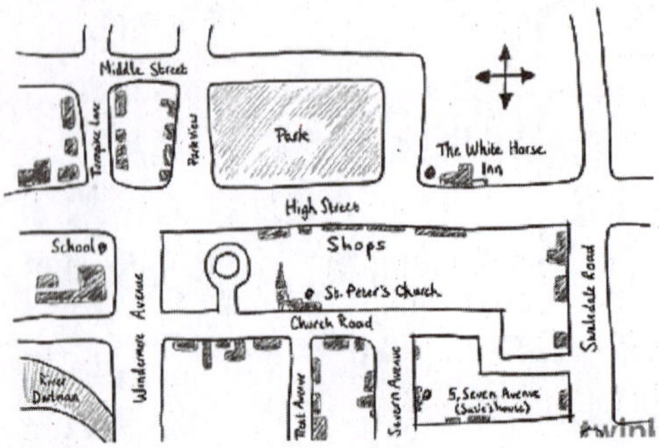

(a) Map
(b) Plan
(c) Sketch
(d) Grid wise map

10. The map that shows the distribution of industries is called a ....
(a) Physical Map
(b) Political Map
(c) Thematic Map
(d) Climatic Map

11. The Survey of India is the national survey and mapping organisation. It was established in the year ....
(a) 1947
(b) 1837
(c) 1767
(d) 1924

MCQs 2 Marks Questions

12. Which of the following statements is incorrect regarding the colour shown in map?
(a) Blue colour is used for showing water bodies.
(b) Brown colour is used for showing mountains.
(c) Pink colour is used for showing plains.
(d) None of the above

13. Read the following statements and select which ones are true (T) and which ones are false (F).
I. Physical map shows the natural features of the Earth.
II. Political maps shows the cities, towns and different states of the world.
III. Maps contain an arrow marked with the letter N at the upper left corner which shows the North direction.

Codes

	I	II	III		I	II	III
(a)	F	T	T	(b)	T	T	F
(c)	F	F	T	(d)	T	F	F

14. Fill in the blanks with appropriate words.
The science of map-making is called ......(A)...... . It is derived from the French word 'carte' which means map and graphic means drawing. Cartographers use the method known as ......(B)...... to show the curved surface on a flat map.

	A	B
(a)	Cartography	map projection
(b)	Cartography	map exaggeration
(c)	Map Analysis	map simplification
(d)	Map Analysis	map simplification

15. Match the following.

	List I (Conventional Symbols)		List II (Meaning)
A.	- - - - - - -	1.	Graveyard
B.	▲	2.	District Border
C.		3.	Unmetalled roads
D.	=======	4.	Mountain

Codes

	A	B	C	D
(a)	2	4	3	1
(b)	2	4	1	3
(c)	2	3	4	1
(d)	2	1	3	4

16. There are two statements marked as Assertion (A) and Reason (R). Mark your answer as per the codes given below.

Assertion (A) Horizontal and vertical lines are drawn on a map, which criss-cross each other and form a network or grid.

Reason (R) Lines are drawn to make it possible to locate a place on a map and the grid provides us with fixed reference points.

Codes

(a) Both A and R are true and R is the correct explanation of A

(b) Both A and R are true, but R is not the correct explanation of A

(c) A is true, but R is false

(d) A is false, but R is true

Darken your choice with HB Pencil

1.	ⓐ ⓑ ⓒ ⓓ	4.	ⓐ ⓑ ⓒ ⓓ	7.	ⓐ ⓑ ⓒ ⓓ	10.	ⓐ ⓑ ⓒ ⓓ	13.	ⓐ ⓑ ⓒ ⓓ	16.	ⓐ ⓑ ⓒ ⓓ
2.	ⓐ ⓑ ⓒ ⓓ	5.	ⓐ ⓑ ⓒ ⓓ	8.	ⓐ ⓑ ⓒ ⓓ	11.	ⓐ ⓑ ⓒ ⓓ	14.	ⓐ ⓑ ⓒ ⓓ		
3.	ⓐ ⓑ ⓒ ⓓ	6.	ⓐ ⓑ ⓒ ⓓ	9.	ⓐ ⓑ ⓒ ⓓ	12.	ⓐ ⓑ ⓒ ⓓ	15.	ⓐ ⓑ ⓒ ⓓ		

Chapter 13

Major Domains of the Earth

MCQs 1 Mark Questions

1. Which is/are the forces that contribute to the formation of landforms on the Earth?
   (a) Internal
   (b) External
   (c) Neither (a) nor (b)
   (d) Both (a) and (b)

2. Complete the given analogy.
   Lithosphere : Solid portion of the Earth : : Hydrosphere :?
   (a) Gaseous layer of the Earth
   (b) Combined zone of land, water and air
   (c) Comprises of water
   (d) Both (b) and (c)

3. The pressure which the air around us exerts on the Earth's surface is called air pressure. It depends on which of the following factors?
   (a) Temperature of air and altitude
   (b) Only altitude
   (c) Only temperature
   (d) Neither temperature nor altitude

4. .... separates North and South America while .... joined them.
   (a) Isthmus of Panama, Panama Canal
   (b) Panama Canal, Isthmus of Panama
   (c) Gulf of Mexico, Puerto Rico Trench
   (d) Puerto Rico Trench, Gulf of Mexico

5. Which of the following is not an Indian research station in Antarctica?
   (a) Alakananda
   (b) Maitri
   (c) Bharti
   (d) Dakshin Gangotri

6. Arrange the oceans in order of decreasing size.
   (a) Pacific, Indian, Southern, Atlantic, Arctic
   (b) Pacific, Southern, Atlantic, Indian, Arctic
   (c) Pacific, Atlantic, Southern, Indian, Arctic
   (d) Pacific, Atlantic, Indian, Southern, Arctic

7. Which of the following water body is a collective extension of the Indian Ocean, Pacific Ocean and Atlantic Ocean?
   (a) Scotia Sea
   (b) Gulf of Guinea
   (c) Southern Ocean
   (d) Kermadec Trench

8. The Pacific Ocean joins the Arctic Ocean through the ....
   (a) Hudson Bay
   (b) Gulf of Alaska
   (c) Atlantic Ocean
   (d) Bering Strait

9. Choose the incorrect pair.

(a) Atlantic Ocean – S shape
(b) Pacific Ocean – Circular in shape
(c) Indian Ocean – Triangular shape
(d) Artic Ocean – L shape

10. Which is the busiest ocean in terms of passenger and cargo traffic?

(a) Pacific (b) Indian
(c) Atlantic (d) Southern

11. Identify the largest river in the world.

(a) Nile River
(b) Ganga
(c) Amazon River
(d) Yangtze River

12. Identify the incorrect statement(s).

(a) All the oceans of the world are connected with each other.
(b) The level of seawater is different everywhere.
(c) Elevation of land is measured from the level of the sea, which is taken as zero.
(d) Both (a) and (b)

13. Complete the given analogy.

Nile : Africa : : ? : South America

(a) Yellow River
(b) Amazon River
(c) Mekong River
(d) Brahmaputra River

MCQs 2 Marks Questions

14. Identify the continent from the following information.

- It is the second largest continent by size and is divided in two equal halves.
- The continent is rich in gold, diamonds and other minerals. It enjoys geographical diversity as it is home to some of the largest landforms on planet.

(a) Europe
(b) Africa
(c) South America
(d) Australia

15. Read the following statements about conventional symbols and select which ones are true (T) and which ones are false (F).

I. North America is second largest continent in the world.
II. Antartica lies completely in Southern hemisphere.
III. Australia is the smallest continent.

	I	II	III
(a)	T	F	F
(b)	F	T	T
(c)	F	F	T
(d)	F	T	F

16. There are two statements marked as Assertion (A) and Reason (R). Mark your answer as per the codes given below.

Assertion (A) Earth's surface is covered with water. Therefore it is called hydrosphere.

Reason (R) More than 71% of the Earth is covered with water.

Codes

(a) Both A and R are true and R is the correct explanation of A

(b) Both A and R are true, but R is not the correct explanation of A

(c) A is true, but R is false

(d) A is false, but R is true

17. Identify the personality from the following information.

- He was an Italian explorer and navigator who completed four voyages across the Atlantic Ocean.
- He arrived on the shores of Americas in 1492 and discovered an entire continent unknown to humanity at that point.

(a) Vasco da Gama

(b) Christopher Columbus

(c) Marco Polo

(d) Amerigo Vespucci

18. Match the following.

List I	List II
A. Lithos	1. Vapour
B. Atmos	2. Water
C. Hudor	3. Life
D. Bios	4. Stone

Codes

	A	B	C	D
(a)	1	2	3	4
(b)	2	3	4	1
(c)	4	1	2	3
(d)	3	2	4	1

Darken your choice with HB Pencil

1.	ⓐ ⓑ ⓒ ⓓ	5.	ⓐ ⓑ ⓒ ⓓ	9.	ⓐ ⓑ ⓒ ⓓ	13.	ⓐ ⓑ ⓒ ⓓ	17.	ⓐ ⓑ ⓒ ⓓ
2.	ⓐ ⓑ ⓒ ⓓ	6.	ⓐ ⓑ ⓒ ⓓ	10.	ⓐ ⓑ ⓒ ⓓ	14.	ⓐ ⓑ ⓒ ⓓ	18.	ⓐ ⓑ ⓒ ⓓ
3.	ⓐ ⓑ ⓒ ⓓ	7.	ⓐ ⓑ ⓒ ⓓ	11.	ⓐ ⓑ ⓒ ⓓ	15.	ⓐ ⓑ ⓒ ⓓ		
4.	ⓐ ⓑ ⓒ ⓓ	8.	ⓐ ⓑ ⓒ ⓓ	12.	ⓐ ⓑ ⓒ ⓓ	16.	ⓐ ⓑ ⓒ ⓓ		

Chapter 14

India : A Geographical Overview

MCQs 1 Mark Questions

1. What does a piece of land surrounded by water on three sides known as?
(a) Bay (b) Gulf
(c) Peninsula (d) Strait

2. Which is the second most populous country of the world?
(a) India (b) China
(c) Pakistan (d) Croatia

3. In which state the Sun rises about two hours earlier in Gujarat?
(a) Kerala
(b) Arunachal Pradesh
(c) Uttarakhand
(d) Odisha

4. Identify the longitude that has been taken as the Indian Standard Time.
(a) 82°30′E (b) 82°30′W
(c) 23°5′E (d) 23°5′W

5. Which among the following rivers does not flow in Uttar Pradesh, India?
(a) Ganga (b) Gomti
(c) Jhelum (d) Yamuna

6. Identify the correct statement(s).
(a) Yamuna is the largest river of India.
(b) Brahmaputra joins Ganga river to form Sunderban Delta.
(c) Both (a) and (b)
(d) None of the above

7. Which two major rivers fall into the Arabian Sea?
(a) Ganga and Brahmaputra
(b) Gomti and Ghaghra
(c) Narmada and Tapi
(d) Kaveri and Krishna

8. Where are the world's highest peaks located?
(a) Middle Himalayan ranges
(b) Greater Himalayas
(c) Shivaliks
(d) None of the above

9. A river or stream which contributes its water to a main river by discharging it into main river from either side is known as ....
(a) Tributary (b) Channel
(c) Drainage (d) Flow

10. Which two rivers form the world's largest delta, the Sundarbans Delta?
(a) Indus and Jhelum
(b) Ganga and Yamuna
(c) Kaveri and Tungabhadra
(d) Ganga and Brahmaputra

11. The West flowing rivers of India drain their water into ....
(a) Bay of Bengal (b) Arabian Sea
(c) Indian Ocean (d) Palk Strait

12. Identify the geographical region of India that provides most fertile land for cultivation.
(a) Great Himalayas
(b) Great Indian Deserts
(c) North Indian Plains
(d) Islands

13. What is the shape of the peninsular plateau?
(a) Triangular (b) Circular
(c) Rectangular (d) Plane

14. Chota Nagpur is rich in which of the following minerals?
(a) Coal, Iron-Ore (b) Zinc, Magnesium
(c) Lead, Gold (d) Uranium, Zinc

15. Andaman and the Nicobar Islands lie in the ....
(a) Gulf of Cambay (b) Bay of Bengal
(c) Arabian Sea (d) Tethys Sea

16. Identify the island of India which is known as the 'Coral island'.
(a) Dharmadam Island
(b) Lakshadweep
(c) Hare Island
(d) Andaman and Nicobar

17. Which of the following countries was not affected by the Tsunami of 2004?
(a) Nepal (b) Indonesia
(c) Thailand (d) India

MCQs 2 Marks Questions

18. Fill in the blanks with the appropriate words.

India has an area of about 3.28 million km sq. The ......(A)...... extent from Ladakh to Kanyakumari is about 3,200 km. The East-West extent from Arunachal Pradesh to Kuchchh is about ......(B)....... .

	A	B
(a)	North- East	25000 km
(b)	North- South	2900 km
(c)	East-West	2000 km
(d)	South- East	1500 km

19. Consider the following statements.
I. All the countries of the world have a single standard time.
II. India is divided into seven time zones.
III. The USA and Canada have seven and six time zones, respectively.

Which of the statements given above is/are correct?
(a) Only I
(b) I and II
(c) Only III
(d) All of the above

20. Match the following.

List I (Landform)	**List II** (Features)
A. Deserts	1. Large stretches of flat land
B. Mountain	2. Elevated flat land
C. Plains	3. Hot and Sandy
D. Plateau	4. Natural elevation of the Earth Surface

	A	B	C	D
(a)	3	4	1	2
(b)	4	1	2	3
(c)	4	2	3	1
(d)	2	1	4	3

21. Identify the mountain ranges A and B given in the map below.

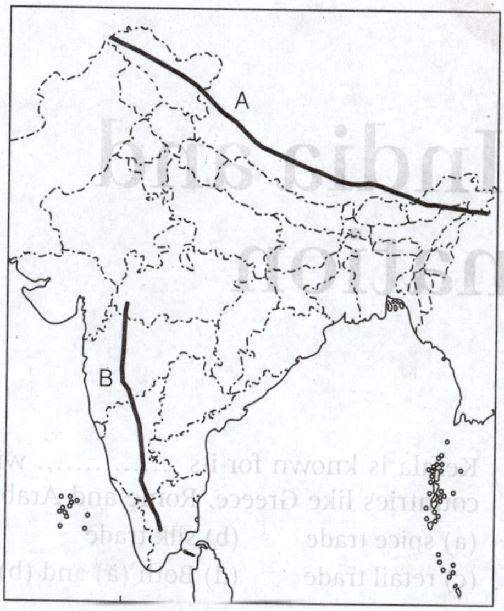

	A	B
(a)	Middle Himalayas	Eastern Ghats
(b)	Great Himalayas	Western Ghats
(c)	Shivaliks	Satpura
(d)	Nilgiris	Deccan Plateau

22. Read the following statements and choose which ones are true (T) and which ones are false (F).

I. From South to North, mainland of India extends between 8°4'N and 37°6'N latitudes.

II. The Shivalik is the Northernmost range of Himalayas.

III. Sri Lanka is separated from India by the Palk Strait.

Codes

	I	II	III		I	II	III
(a)	F	T	F	(b)	F	T	T
(c)	T	F	T	(d)	T	T	F

23. There are two statements marked as Assertion (A) and Reason (R). Mark your answer as per the codes given below.

Assertion (A) Northern Indian plains are formed by the alluvial deposits laid down by the rivers.

Reason (R) There is high concentration of population in Northern Indian plains.

Codes

(a) Both A and R are true and R is the correct explanation of A

(b) Both A and R are true, but R is not the correct explanation of A

(c) A is true, but R is false

(d) R is true, but A is false

24. Arrange the following ranges from North to South.

A. Himadri B. Vindhyas

C. Shivalik D. Aravali

Codes

(a) B-C-D-A (b) A-C-D-B

(c) A-D-C-B (d) A-B-C-D

Darken your choice with HB Pencil

1. (a) (b) (c) (d)	5. (a) (b) (c) (d)	9. (a) (b) (c) (d)	13. (a) (b) (c) (d)	17. (a) (b) (c) (d)	21. (a) (b) (c) (d)
2. (a) (b) (c) (d)	6. (a) (b) (c) (d)	10. (a) (b) (c) (d)	14. (a) (b) (c) (d)	18. (a) (b) (c) (d)	22. (a) (b) (c) (d)
3. (a) (b) (c) (d)	7. (a) (b) (c) (d)	11. (a) (b) (c) (d)	15. (a) (b) (c) (d)	19. (a) (b) (c) (d)	23. (a) (b) (c) (d)
4. (a) (b) (c) (d)	8. (a) (b) (c) (d)	12. (a) (b) (c) (d)	16. (a) (b) (c) (d)	20. (a) (b) (c) (d)	24. (a) (b) (c) (d)

Chapter 15

Diversity in India and Discrimination

MCQs 1 Mark Questions

1. India is a country of various religions, castes, languages and cultures and still we live in harmony with each other. It means India has ....

(a) unity in diversity (b) one common rule
(c) esprit de corps (d) full faith

2. Identify the famous personality who coined the phrase 'unity in diversity' to describe India.

(a) Mahatma Gandhi
(b) Sardar Vallabhbhai Patel
(c) Subhash Chandra Bose
(d) Pt Jawaharlal Nehru

3. Choose the incorrect statement from the given options.

(a) A stereotype is created when we fix people into one image.
(b) Stereotypes helps us to analyse special qualities and skills of each person.
(c) Stereotypes fit large numbers of people into only one pattern.
(d) Stereotypes affect all of us as they prevent us from doing certain things that we might otherwise be good at.

4. Identify the State of India in which boat races (Vallam Kali) are organised.

(a) Jharkhand (b) Jammu and Kashmir
(c) Kerala (d) Andhra Pradesh

Kerala is known for its .... with countries like Greece, Rome and Arabia.

(a) spice trade (b) silk trade
(c) retail trade (d) Both (a) and (b)

6. What is the reason for discrimination and inequality in India?

(a) Attitude (b) Poverty
(c) Caste system (d) Diversity

7. Which of the following examples shows a form of discrimination?

(a) Being made to sit separately in the classroom because of one's background.
(b) Lower caste people were not allowed to enter the homes of upper caste.
(c) Boys are more rational while girls are more emotional and creative.
(d) Both (a) and (b)

8. To judge other people negatively or see them as inferior is known as ....

(a) bullying (b) prejudice
(c) stratification (d) None of these

9. Identify the main cause for non-attendance of Muslim girls in school.

(a) Poor infrastructure
(b) Religion
(c) Poverty
(d) Lack of government initiatives

10. Complete the given analogy.

Stereotype : Discrimination : : Dalit : ?

(a) Place (b) Caste
(c) Religion (d) Gender

MCQs 2 Marks Questions

11. There are two statements marked as Assertion (A) and Reason (R). Mark your answer as per the codes given below.

Assertion (A) The real purpose of the Constitution was to ensure proper functioning of the government after independence.

Reason (R) The equality of all persons was seen as a key value that would unite all the Indians in years to come.

Codes

(a) Both A and R are true and R is the correct explanation of A
(b) Both A and R are true, but R is not the correct explanation of A
(c) A is true, but R is false
(d) A is false, but R is true

12. On the basis of information given below, identify the states.

I. It does not receive any rain and is covered in snow for a large part of the year. It also called Little Tibet.

II. It is a state in the South-West corner of India. A number of spices like pepper, cloves and cardamoms are grown on the hills.

	I	II
(a)	Haryana	Karnataka
(b)	Ladakh	Kerala
(c)	Uttarakhand	Tamil Nadu
(d)	Mizoram	Manipur

13. Match the following.

List I		List II	
A.	Cheena-vala	1.	Local version of Tibetan national epic
B.	Cheenachatti	2.	Fishing net
C.	Kesar Saga	3.	Utensil

Codes

	A	B	C		A	B	C
(a)	3	2	1	(b)	3	1	2
(c)	1	2	3	(d)	2	3	1

14. Arrange the following events of Indian history in chronological order.

I. India gained Independence
II. Birth of Bhimrao Ambedkar
III. Jallianwala Bagh Massacre

Codes

(a) III, II, I (b) II, III, I
(c) I, II, III (d) III, I, II

15. Read the following statements and choose which ones are true (T) and which ones are false (F).

I. The Discovery of India was written by Jawaharlal Nehru.
II. Jawaharlal Nehru delivered the speech on the eve of Independence.
III. According to Jawaharlal Nehru, Indian unity is not something imposed from the outside but rather it was something deeper.

Codes

	I	II	III		I	II	III
(a)	F	F	T	(b)	F	T	F
(c)	T	T	T	(d)	T	F	F

Darken your choice with HB Pencil

1.	ⓐ ⓑ ⓒ ⓓ	4.	ⓐ ⓑ ⓒ ⓓ	7.	ⓐ ⓑ ⓒ ⓓ	10.	ⓐ ⓑ ⓒ ⓓ	13.	ⓐ ⓑ ⓒ ⓓ
2.	ⓐ ⓑ ⓒ ⓓ	5.	ⓐ ⓑ ⓒ ⓓ	8.	ⓐ ⓑ ⓒ ⓓ	11.	ⓐ ⓑ ⓒ ⓓ	14.	ⓐ ⓑ ⓒ ⓓ
3.	ⓐ ⓑ ⓒ ⓓ	6.	ⓐ ⓑ ⓒ ⓓ	9.	ⓐ ⓑ ⓒ ⓓ	12.	ⓐ ⓑ ⓒ ⓓ	15.	ⓐ ⓑ ⓒ ⓓ

Chapter 16

Government

MCQs 1 Mark Questions

1. How the power of the government gets limited in a democracy?
   (a) By regular elections
   (b) By public protests
   (c) By social movements
   (d) Through discussions

2. What happens when people of different cultures, religions or economic backgrounds do not get along with each other or when they are discriminated against?
   (a) War
   (b) Marriage
   (c) Conflict
   (d) Election

3. Complete the given analogy.
   Monarchy : King make laws : : ? : Government make laws
   (a) Democracy
   (b) Anarchy
   (c) Totalitarianism
   (d) Both (a) and (b)

4. What does the term 'suffrage' usually mean?
   (a) Suffering
   (b) Right to enforce decision
   (c) Right to Vote
   (d) Right to take action

5. In a monarchy, the power to make decisions and run the government rests with ....
   (a) Prime Minister (b) Industrialists
   (c) King/Queen (d) Military Commander

6. Which of the following institutions are part of the government?
   (a) Supreme Court
   (b) Indian Railways
   (c) Bharat Petroleum
   (d) All of the above

7. What does the term 'Universal Adult Franchise' mean?
   (a) All adults are allowed to work.
   (b) All adults are eligible for marriage.
   (c) All adults in the country are allowed to vote.
   (d) None of the above

8. Identify the institution of Government of India from the image given below.

(a) Supreme Court of India
(b) Sansad Bhavan
(c) President House
(d) White House

9. Which among the following countries gave its women Right to Vote in 1920?
(a) USA
(b) Russia
(c) India
(d) China

10. What was the name of the Journal published by Mahatma Gandhi?
(a) Discovery of India
(b) Satyarth Prakash
(c) Young India
(d) Harijan

11. Choose the incorrect statement about Democracy.
(a) Government gives power to the people.
(b) People vote for particular person and elect them.
(c) Government explains its action to people.
(d) None of the above.

MCQs 2 Marks Questions

12. Consider the following statements and select the incorrect statement.
(a) In India, before independence, only a small minority was allowed to vote.
(b) In a representative democracy, people do participate directly.
(c) Women and poor were not allowed to participate in elections during the earlier times.
(d) Gandhiji demanded that all adults must have the Right to Vote.

13. Read the following statements and choose which ones are true (T) and which ones are false (F).
I. In a monarchy, the country's citizens are allowed to elect whoever they want.
II. In a democracy, a king has absolute powers to rule the country.
III. In a monarchy, people can raise questions about the decisions the monarch takes.
IV. People have the power to elect their leaders in a democracy.

	I	II	III	IV		I	II	III	IV
(a)	F	T	T	F	(b)	F	F	F	T
(c)	T	F	T	T	(d)	T	T	F	T

14. Fill in the blanks with appropriate words.
India is a ……(A)…… . The main feature of this form of government is that the people have the power to elect their leaders. Such governments are usually referred to as ……(B)…… .

	A	B
(a)	autocracy	Good Rule
(b)	democracy	Representative Democracies
(c)	monarchy	Ram Rajya
(d)	dictatorship	Team

15. Match the following.

List I (Year)	**List II** (Event)
A. 1920	1. Kashmir was divided into UTs
B. 2019	2. UK women got Right to Vote
C. 2014	3. Telangana was created
D. 1928	4. USA women got Right to Vote

Codes

	A	B	C	D		A	B	C	D
(a)	3	4	1	2	(b)	4	1	3	2
(c)	4	2	3	1	(d)	2	3	4	1

16. On the given map of India, identify the place where the Parliament of India is situated.

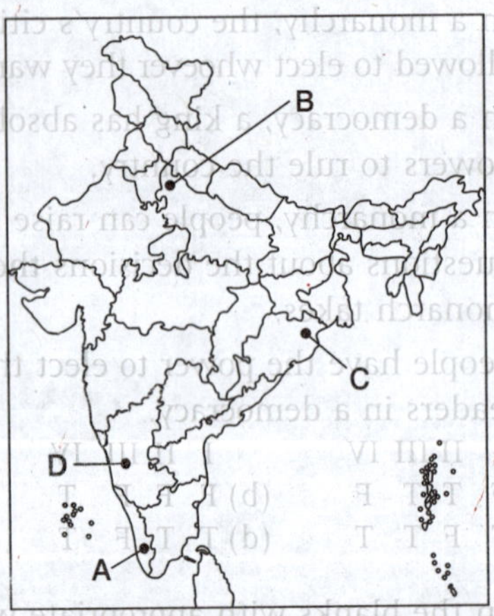

(a) A (b) B (c) C (d) D

17. Consider the following statements.

I. Government protects boundaries of country and maintain peaceful relations.

II. Government takes actions on social issues.

Which of the statements given above is/are correct?

(a) Only I

(b) Only II

(c) Both I and II

(d) Neither I nor II

18. There are two statements marked as a Assertion (A) and Reason (R). Mark your answer as per the codes given below.

Assertion (A) The government plays an important part in resolving conflicts.

Reason (R) It formulates guidelines for certain religious sects to follow while taking out peaceful processions.

Codes

(a) Both A and R are true and R is the correct explanation of A

(b) Both A and R are true, but R is not the correct explanation of A

(c) A is true, but R is false

(d) A is false, but R is true

Darken your choice with HB Pencil

1.	ⓐ ⓑ ⓒ ⓓ	4.	ⓐ ⓑ ⓒ ⓓ	7.	ⓐ ⓑ ⓒ ⓓ	10.	ⓐ ⓑ ⓒ ⓓ	13.	ⓐ ⓑ ⓒ ⓓ	16.	ⓐ ⓑ ⓒ ⓓ
2.	ⓐ ⓑ ⓒ ⓓ	5.	ⓐ ⓑ ⓒ ⓓ	8.	ⓐ ⓑ ⓒ ⓓ	11.	ⓐ ⓑ ⓒ ⓓ	14.	ⓐ ⓑ ⓒ ⓓ	17.	ⓐ ⓑ ⓒ ⓓ
3.	ⓐ ⓑ ⓒ ⓓ	6.	ⓐ ⓑ ⓒ ⓓ	9.	ⓐ ⓑ ⓒ ⓓ	12.	ⓐ ⓑ ⓒ ⓓ	15.	ⓐ ⓑ ⓒ ⓓ	18.	ⓐ ⓑ ⓒ ⓓ

Chapter 17

Panchayati Raj & Rural-Urban Administration

MCQs 1 Mark Questions

1. Where do people directly participate and seek answers from their elected representatives?
   (a) Gram Sabha
   (b) Parliament
   (c) Gram Panchayat
   (d) None of the above

2. Every Village Panchayat is divided into smaller areas known as ....
   (a) Ward (b) Block
   (c) Zila (d) Unit

3. Who elects the Panchayat President (Sarpanch)?
   (a) Mayors of the city
   (b) Members of Gram Sabha
   (c) All People of village
   (d) All of the above

4. ...... is responsible for calling the meeting of the Gram Sabha and Gram Panchayat and keeping a record of the proceedings.
   (a) Gram Pradhan
   (b) Panchayat Assistant
   (c) Panchayat Secretary
   (d) BDO

5. Which award is given to Panchs for the excellent work done by them in the Panchayat?
   (a) Nobel Prize
   (b) Bharat Ratna
   (c) Oscar
   (d) Nirmal Gram Puraskar

6. Whose main work is to measure land and keep land records?
   (a) Patwari (b) Prime Minister
   (c) SHO (d) Sarpanch

7. At which level does Zila Parishad actually make development plans?
   (a) District level (b) Panchayat level
   (c) Block level (d) Government level

8. Who among the following ensure that the farmers can easily obtain a copy of their record?
   (a) Patwaris
   (b) Tehsildars
   (c) District Collector
   (d) Panchayat President

9. Which of the following terms is/are used for Patwari?
   (a) Lekhpal (b)Karamchari
   (c) Kanungo (d) All of these

10. Who is responsible for providing basic amenities of school, street lights and hospitals in big cities?
(a) Municipal Administrator
(b) Sarpanch
(c) Municipal Corporation
(d) Chief Minister

11. All the developmental decisions in a Municipal Corporation are made by ....
(a) Sarpanch (b) Prime Minister
(c) People of the city (d) Ward Councillors

12. Complete the given analogy.
Big cities : Municipal Corporation :: Small cities : ?
(a) Municipal Council (b) Parliament
(c) Gram Sabha (d) Ward

13. Government of India launched the Swachh Bharat Mission on the birthday of ....
(a) Narendra Modi (b) Jawaharlal Nehru
(c) Mahatma Gandhi (d) APJ Abdul Kalam

14. Identify the incorrect option about the objective of Swachh Bharat Mission.
(a) Eradicating open defecation
(b) Creating employment
(c) Constructing toilets
(d) Creating a clean India

15. Which of the following is the process of converting waste materials into new materials and objects?
(a) Manufacturing (b) Recycling
(c) Taxation (d) Repurpose

16. Identify the reason for which Gangubai is loved and respected by the people.
(a) She was an active citizen
(b) She was a protestor
(c) She helped the poor
(d) None of the above

17. In the given image, process of recycling is being performed by a person. Which of the following items can be recycled?

(a) Metal and glass
(b) Rags and cloth material
(c) Coffee cups
(d) Used napkins

MCQs 2 Marks Questions

18. With reference to the Panchayati Raj Institutions, which of the following statements is incorrect?
(a) The Gram Sabha is a meeting of all adults who live in the area covered by a Panchayat.
(b) This could be only one village or a few villages.
(c) Anyone who is 21 years old or more and has the Right to Vote is a member of the Gram Sabha.
(d) The Panchs and the Sarpanchs form the Gram Panchayat.

19. Read the following functions of a Gram Sabha and select the correct option.
I. It is the place where all plans for the work of the Gram Panchayat are placed before the people.
II. Gram Sabha encourages Panchayat in doing wrong things like misusing money or favouring certain people.

Codes
(a) Only I (b) Only II
(c) I and II (d) None of these

20. There are two statements marked as Assertion (A) and Reason (R). Mark your answer as per the codes given below.

Assertion (A) Panchayati Raj System is a process through which people participate in their own government.

Reason (R) The Panch and the Gram Panchayat are answerable to the Gram Sabha because the members of the Gram Sabha elected them.

Codes

(a) Both A and R are true and R is the correct explanation of A

(b) Both A and R are true, but R is not the correct explanation of A

(c) A is true, but R is false

(d) A is false, but R is true

21. Consider the list given below and choose the correct option about the functions of a Gram Panchayat.

I. Construction and maintenance of water sources

II. Maintenance of school building

III. Collecting local taxes

IV. Executing employment generation schemes

Codes

(a) I, II and III (b) II, III and IV

(c) I, III and IV (d) All of these

22. Read the following statements and choose which ones are true (T) and which ones are false (F).

I. The work of Gram Panchayat has to be approved by the State Government.

II. Gram Sabha levies and collects local taxes.

III. Development committees can be formed by Gram Sabha.

Codes

	I	II	III
(a)	T	F	T
(b)	F	F	T
(c)	T	T	F
(d)	F	T	F

23. Consider the following statements about the Ward Councillors.

I. In a Municipal Corporation, the Ward Councillors are the elected members.

II. Government of the State appoints people as the Ward Councillors in a Municipal Corporation.

Which of the statements given above is/are correct?

(a) Only I (b) Only II

(c) Both I and II (d) Neither I nor II

24. Read the following statements and choose which ones are true (T) and which ones are false (F).

I. There is a healthy mix of elections and nominations in a Municipal Corporation.

II. Municipalities have a term of only 4 years.

III. Ward Councillors form committees to decide and debate issues.

Codes

	I	II	III		I	II	III
(a)	T	T	F	(b)	T	F	T
(c)	F	T	F	(d)	F	F	T

Darken your choice with HB Pencil

1. ⓐ ⓑ ⓒ ⓓ	5. ⓐ ⓑ ⓒ ⓓ	9. ⓐ ⓑ ⓒ ⓓ	13. ⓐ ⓑ ⓒ ⓓ	17. ⓐ ⓑ ⓒ ⓓ	21. ⓐ ⓑ ⓒ ⓓ
2. ⓐ ⓑ ⓒ ⓓ	6. ⓐ ⓑ ⓒ ⓓ	10. ⓐ ⓑ ⓒ ⓓ	14. ⓐ ⓑ ⓒ ⓓ	18. ⓐ ⓑ ⓒ ⓓ	22. ⓐ ⓑ ⓒ ⓓ
3. ⓐ ⓑ ⓒ ⓓ	7. ⓐ ⓑ ⓒ ⓓ	11. ⓐ ⓑ ⓒ ⓓ	15. ⓐ ⓑ ⓒ ⓓ	19. ⓐ ⓑ ⓒ ⓓ	23. ⓐ ⓑ ⓒ ⓓ
4. ⓐ ⓑ ⓒ ⓓ	8. ⓐ ⓑ ⓒ ⓓ	12. ⓐ ⓑ ⓒ ⓓ	16. ⓐ ⓑ ⓒ ⓓ	20. ⓐ ⓑ ⓒ ⓓ	24. ⓐ ⓑ ⓒ ⓓ

Chapter 18

Rural and Urban Livelihood

MCQs 1 Mark Questions

1. What is the process of removal of unwanted plants that grow in-between crops called?
(a) Harvesting (b) Transplanting
(c) Weeding (d) Farming

2. In which form of cultivation the land on a hill slope is made into flat plots and carved out in steps?
(a) Jhum cultivation
(b) Indigo farming
(c) Terrace cultivation
(d) Forest farming

3. People of Chakhesang community belong to which state?
(a) Gujarat (b) Himachal Pradesh
(c) Mizoram (d) Nagaland

4. The authority that issues a license to the permanent shops is the ....
(a) Parliament of India
(b) Municipal Corporation
(c) Municipal Authority
(d) None of the above

5. Name the kind of workers who get the medical facilities by their employer.
(a) Casual workers
(b) Agriculture labourers
(c) Permanent employees
(d) Street vendors

6. Identify the incorrect statement(s) from the following.
(a) Street vending is viewed as an obstruction to traffic.
(b) Street vending is now recognised as a right of people to earn livelihood.
(c) Both (a) and (b)
(d) None of the above

7. Which among the following activities is/are performed by rural people to support their livelihood?
(a) Fishing (b) Collecting honey
(c) Animal husbandry (d) All of these

8. ...... is a centralised office that deals with problems and questions that customers have regarding goods and services.
(a) Customer Care Office
(b) Call Centre
(c) Home Ministry
(d) None of the above

9. Choose the correct statement(s) from the options given below.
(a) Rural Employment Generation Programme is a scheme which is launched by the Central Government.
(b) It provides self employment opportunities in small towns and rural areas.
(c) Both (a) and (b)
(d) None of the above

10. Sudha gets a regular salary every month and she can expect her job to continue for a long period of time. Identify the type of job in which Sudha is employed.

(a) Daily wage worker
(b) Temporary employee
(c) Permanent employee
(d) None of the above

MCQs 2 Marks Questions

11. Consider the following statements and select the incorrect statement.

(a) Working on farms involves operations such as sowing, weeding and harvesting.
(b) Farmers depend upon nature for the growth of crops.
(c) Small farmers find enough work to keep them employed throughout the year.
(d) Rural people in different regions grow different crops.

12. Read the following statements and choose which ones are true (T) and which ones are false (F).

I. In India, most of the farmers are either small farmers or money lenders.
II. Landless labourers have seasonal jobs.
III. The rich farmers work on the land themselves.

Codes

	I	II	III		I	II	III
(a)	F	F	F	(b)	F	T	F
(c)	T	T	T	(d)	T	F	T

13. There are two statements marked as Assertion (A) and Reason (R). Mark your answer as per the codes given below.

Assertion (A) Agriculture and employment are inversely proportional to each other.

Reason (R) Low productivity in the agriculture sector and lack of transition to other sectors plays a pivotal role in unemployment.

Codes

(a) Both A and R are true and R is the correct explanation of A
(b) Both A and R are true, but R is not the correct explanation of A
(c) A is true, but R is false
(d) A is fals, but R is true

14. Match the following.

List I (Month)	List II (Cropping activity of Paddy)
A. June-July	1. Harvesting
B. August	2. Preparing Saplings
C. September	3. Weeding
D. November	4. Transplanting

Codes

	A	B	C	D		A	B	C	D
(a)	3	4	1	2	(b)	4	1	2	3
(c)	4	2	3	1	(d)	2	4	3	1

15. Consider the following statements with reference to Call Centres.

I. Call Centres provide high salary and security to their employees.
II. India is a hub for all types of Call Centres.

Which of the statements given above is/are correct?

(a) Only I (b) Only II
(c) Both I and II (d) Neither I nor II

Darken your choice with HB Pencil

1.	ⓐ ⓑ ⓒ ⓓ	4.	ⓐ ⓑ ⓒ ⓓ	7.	ⓐ ⓑ ⓒ ⓓ	10.	ⓐ ⓑ ⓒ ⓓ	13.	ⓐ ⓑ ⓒ ⓓ
2.	ⓐ ⓑ ⓒ ⓓ	5.	ⓐ ⓑ ⓒ ⓓ	8.	ⓐ ⓑ ⓒ ⓓ	11.	ⓐ ⓑ ⓒ ⓓ	14.	ⓐ ⓑ ⓒ ⓓ
3.	ⓐ ⓑ ⓒ ⓓ	6.	ⓐ ⓑ ⓒ ⓓ	9.	ⓐ ⓑ ⓒ ⓓ	12.	ⓐ ⓑ ⓒ ⓓ	15.	ⓐ ⓑ ⓒ ⓓ

Practice Set 01

Time : 60 Mins. Max. Marks : 60

General Instructions

1. This question paper contains 50 questions.
2. All questions are compulsory. There is no negative marking.
3. Q. No. 1 to 40 are of 1 mark each and Q. No. 41 to 50 are of 2 marks each.
4. Use HB pencil / Blue ball point pen to mark your choice of answer by darkening the circles on the OMR Sheet.

MCQs 1 Mark Questions

1. On which river bank did the people live along in the ancient time?
(a) Ganga
(b) Narmada
(c) Sutlej
(d) None of the above

2. Which of the two rivers are mentioned in the Rigveda that were worshipped as goddesses?
(a) Ganga and Yamuna
(b) Saraswati and Brahmaputra
(c) Beas and Sutlej
(d) All of the above

3. Identify the name of the sacred book of the Hindus which is a part of the great epic, Mahabharata.
(a) Vedas (b) Ramayana
(c) Gita (d) Purana

4. Which one of the following sites was first to discover in the Indus Valley Civilisation?
(a) Mohenjo-daro
(b) Kalibangan
(c) Harappa
(d) Lothal

5. Which of the following crops is/are grown during Janapadas?
(a) Mustard
(b) Barley
(c) Pulses
(d) All of the above

6. Which term best describes the map showing natural features of the Earth such as mountains, rivers, oceans and so on?
(a) Conventional map
(b) Political map
(c) Physical map
(d) Thematic map

7. The .... may have a small summit and a broad base. It is considerably higher than the surrounding area.
(a) plateaus
(b) mountains
(c) plains
(d) delta

8. How was street vending looked upon?
(a) Street vending looked upon only as an obstruction to traffic
(b) Street vending looked upon to people walking.
(c) Both (a) and (b)
(d) None of the above

9. Measuring land and keeping land records is the main work of this officer. She/he is known by different names in different States. Identify the designation of this officer.

(a) Legal Advisor (b) Advocate
(c) Patwari (d) None of these

10. The given picture shows an old item, which was used about 2500 years ago. The picture signifies which of the following articles?

(a) A statue (b) An old silver coin
(c) A stamp (d) None of these

11. In India, we speak different languages, have various types of food, celebrate different festivals and practice different religions. But we do many things that are similar except that we do them in different ways.
Identify the term which best signifies the given information.

(a) Unity in India
(b) Diversity in India
(c) Unity in Diversity
(d) None of the above

12. The period of rotation is known as the ....

(a) Lunar day
(b) Earth day
(c) Solar day
(d) None of the above

13. How does internal process of Earth affects the Earth surface?

(a) Upliftment of the Earth's surface at several places.
(b) Sinking of the Earth's surface at several places.
(c) Continuous wearing down and rebuilding of the land surface
(d) Both (a) and (b)

14. What is a meeting of all adults who live in the area covered by a Panchayat called?

(a) Gram Parishad
(b) Gram Sabha
(c) Zila Parishad
(d) None of the above

15. A special tank which is also called 'Great Bath' is found in which of the following Harappan cities?

(a) Harappa
(b) Sokhta Koh
(c) Surkotada
(d) Mohenjo-daro

16. The full Moon occurs only once in a ....

(a) year
(b) month
(c) weak
(d) Both (a) and (b)

17. Complete the given analogy.
Poornima : Full Moon : : ? : New Moon

(a) Amavasya
(b) Shukla Paksh
(c) Krishna Paksh
(d) None of the above

18. Identify the incorrect statement.

(a) Tropic of Cancer lies at 12½°S.
(b) Latitudes are measured in degrees.
(c) Globe is a true model of the Earth
(d) None of the above

19. How did the Dasa Karnataka earn their living in the Ancient India?

(a) By performing art
(b) By fighting in the army
(c) By working in other's field
(d) Both (a) and (b)

20. Which of the following best describes the shape of the Earth?

(a) A sphere which bulges at the poles and flattens at the centre.
(b) A sphere which bulges at the poles and at the centre.
(c) A sphere which flattens at the poles and bulges at the centre.
(d) A perfect sphere.

21. When large scale areas like countries or continents are shown on a small map, it is known as ....

(a) near scale map
(b) short scale map
(c) small area map
(d) small scale map

22. In India, the government works at which of the following levels?

(a) Local level
(b) National level
(c) State level
(d) All of the above

23. On which level does Indian government take decision to maintain peaceful relation with Russia?

(a) Local level
(b) State level
(c) Central level
(d) None of the above

24. Identify the incorrectly matched pair.

(a) Purana Qila – Delhi
(b) Golden Pagoda – Arunachal Pradesh
(c) Atranjikhera – Etah
(d) Kosala – Madras

25. Complete the given analogy.

Sabha : An assembly of Brahmin land owners :: Nagaram : ?

(a) A village assembly where the land owners were not Jainas
(b) A village assembly where the land owners were not Brahmins
(c) An organisation of merchants
(d) None of the above

26. The circle that divides the day from night on globe is called ....

(a) orbital plane
(b) axis
(c) circle of illumination
(d) elliptical orbit

27. The people of Chakhesang Community belong to which of the following states of India?

(a) Assam (b) Tripura
(c) Nagaland (d) Odisha

28. .... is the process in which people grew plant and look often animal.

(a) Farming
(b) Herding
(c) Domestication
(d) Microliths

29. Complete the given analogy.

Orbital plane : The plane formed by the orbit : : ? : The circle that divides the Globe into day and night

(a) Circle of darkness
(b) Circle of day and night
(c) Circle of illumination
(d) None of the above

30. In which state(s) of India, is there less distance between home and school?

(a) Rajasthan
(b) Kerala
(c) Mumbai
(d) All of the above

31. Identify the agency, which replaces the broken street collects the garbage, provides water supply and keeps the market clean.
(a) Gram Sabha
(b) District Council
(c) Municipal Corporation
(d) Panchayat Samiti

32. What is the main cause for non-attendance of Muslim girls in school?
(a) Religion
(b) Poverty
(c) Poor infrastructure
(d) Lack of government initiative

33. What is a needle fixed through the Globe in a tilted manner called?
(a) Longitude (b) Orbit
(c) Axis (d) Latitude

34. For which of the following purposes the hunter-gatherers used the stone tools?
(a) To cut meat and bone
(b) To scrape bark
(c) To chop fruit and roots
(d) All of the above

35. Who among the following was the founder of the Mauryan Empire?
(a) Ashoka (b) Chandragupta
(c) Chanakya (d) Bindusara

36. Identify the river which is the world's longest river which flows through Africa Continent.
(a) Amazon river (b) Tigris river
(c) Nile river (d) Huang He river

37. In which part of the Indian sub-continent, the village headman was known as the Grama Bhojaka?
(a) Southern (b) Northern
(c) Eastern (d) Western

38. What is/are the feature(s) of Jupiter?
(a) It is covered in swirling cloud stripes.
(b) It is a gas giant and doesn't have a solid surface.
(c) It has big storms like the Great Red Spot.
(d) All of the above

39. It is the only continent through which the Tropic of Cancer, the Equator and the Tropic of Capricorn pass. Identify the continent from the given options.
(a) South America
(b) Asia
(c) Africa
(d) Antarctica

40. Which of the following countries has maximum time zones in the world?
(a) Canada
(b) Russia
(c) USA
(d) England

MCQs 2 Marks Questions

41. There are two statements marked as Assertion (A) and Reason (R). Mark your answer as per the codes given below.

Assertion (A) Hunter-gatherers moved from place to place.

Reason (R) If hunter-gatherers had stayed at one place for a long time, they would have eaten up all the available plant and animal resources.

Codes
(a) Both A and R are true and R is the correct explanation of A
(b) Both A and R are true, but R is not the correct explanation of A
(c) A is true, but R is false
(d) A is false, but R is true

42. Read the given statements and select which ones are true (T) and which ones are false (F).

I. The government has the job of protecting the boundaries of the country and maintaining peaceful relations with other countries.

II. The government is responsible for ensuring that all its citizens have enough to eat and have good health facilities.

III. When there are natural disasters like the tsunami or an earthquake, it is the government that mainly organises aid and assistance for the affected people.

Codes

	I	II	III		I	II	III
(a)	T	F	F	(b)	T	T	F
(c)	T	T	T	(d)	F	T	F

43. Match the following.

List I	List II
A. Largest continent in the world	1. Africa
B. Second largest continent in the world	2. North America
C. Third largest continent in the world	3. Australia
D. Smallest continent in the world	4. Asia

Codes

	A	B	C	D		A	B	C	D
(a)	1	2	3	4	(b)	4	1	2	3
(c)	3	4	1	2	(d)	3	1	2	4

44. Consider the following statements about the Indus Valley Civilisation.

I. Cities were divided into two parts only.

II. Eastern part was smaller, but higher is called Citadel.

III. Western part was bigger, but the lower is called the lower town.

Which of the above statements is/are correct?

(a) Only I

(b) I and II

(c) II and III

(d) None of the above

45. There are two statement marked as Assertion (A) and Reason (R). Mark your answer as per the codes given below.

Assertion (A) Venus is considered as the Earth's twin.

Reason (R) Its size and shape are similar to that of the Earth.

Codes

(a) Both A and R are true and R is the correct explanation of A

(b) Both A and R are true, but R is not the correct explanation of A

(c) A is true, but R is false

(d) A is false, but R is true

46. Consider the following statements.

I. Prejudice means to judge other people negatively or see them as inferior.

II. When we think that only one particular way is the best and right way to do things, we often end up not respecting others, who may prefer to do things differently.

III. If we think English is the best language and other languages are not important, we are judging these other languages negatively.

Which of the following statements is/are correct?

(a) Only I

(b) I and II

(c) I and III

(d) All of the above

47. Identify the important centres of Mauryan Empire marked as A and B on the given outline map of Indian sub-continent.

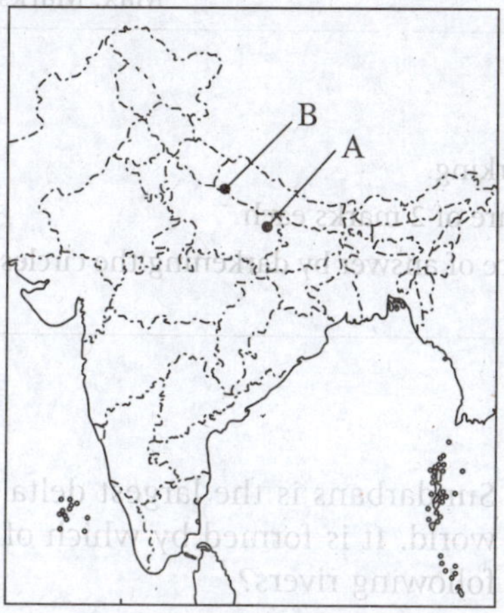

	A	B
(a)	Sopara	Maski
(b)	Lumbini	Pataliputra
(c)	Topara	Meerut
(d)	Allahabad	Sarnath

48. There are two statements marked as Assertion (A) and Reason (R). Mark your answer as per the codes given below.

Assertion (A) The Arabian Sea in the West, the Bay of Bengal in the East and the Indian ocean in the South wash the shores of the Indian Peninsula.

Reason (R) The Peninsula is a piece of land that is surrounded by water on three sides.

Codes

(a) Both A and R are true and R is the correct explanation of A

(b) Both A and R are true, but R is not the correct explanation of A

(c) A is true, but R is false

(d) A is false, but R is true

49. Identify the personality from the information given below.

- He was an ambassador, who was sent to the court of Chandragupta by the Greek ruler of West Asia named Seleucus Nicator.
- He wrote an account about what he saw in the Indian sub-continent.

(a) Vasco da Gama
(b) Megasthenes
(c) Eratosthenes
(d) Christopher Columbus

50. Consider the following statements and choose the correct option.

I. Patwari is responsible for organising the collection of land revenue from the farmers.

II. Patwari provides information to the government about the crops grown in a measured area.

III. It is the responsibility of the Patwari to regularly update the records.

Codes

(a) Only I (b) I and II
(c) II and III (d) All of these

Darken your choice with HB Pencil

1.	ⓐ ⓑ ⓒ ⓓ	10.	ⓐ ⓑ ⓒ ⓓ	19.	ⓐ ⓑ ⓒ ⓓ	28.	ⓐ ⓑ ⓒ ⓓ	37.	ⓐ ⓑ ⓒ ⓓ	46.	ⓐ ⓑ ⓒ ⓓ
2.	ⓐ ⓑ ⓒ ⓓ	11.	ⓐ ⓑ ⓒ ⓓ	20.	ⓐ ⓑ ⓒ ⓓ	29.	ⓐ ⓑ ⓒ ⓓ	38.	ⓐ ⓑ ⓒ ⓓ	47.	ⓐ ⓑ ⓒ ⓓ
3.	ⓐ ⓑ ⓒ ⓓ	12.	ⓐ ⓑ ⓒ ⓓ	21.	ⓐ ⓑ ⓒ ⓓ	30.	ⓐ ⓑ ⓒ ⓓ	39.	ⓐ ⓑ ⓒ ⓓ	48.	ⓐ ⓑ ⓒ ⓓ
4.	ⓐ ⓑ ⓒ ⓓ	13.	ⓐ ⓑ ⓒ ⓓ	22.	ⓐ ⓑ ⓒ ⓓ	31.	ⓐ ⓑ ⓒ ⓓ	40.	ⓐ ⓑ ⓒ ⓓ	49.	ⓐ ⓑ ⓒ ⓓ
5.	ⓐ ⓑ ⓒ ⓓ	14.	ⓐ ⓑ ⓒ ⓓ	23.	ⓐ ⓑ ⓒ ⓓ	32.	ⓐ ⓑ ⓒ ⓓ	41.	ⓐ ⓑ ⓒ ⓓ	50.	ⓐ ⓑ ⓒ ⓓ
6.	ⓐ ⓑ ⓒ ⓓ	15.	ⓐ ⓑ ⓒ ⓓ	24.	ⓐ ⓑ ⓒ ⓓ	33.	ⓐ ⓑ ⓒ ⓓ	42.	ⓐ ⓑ ⓒ ⓓ		
7.	ⓐ ⓑ ⓒ ⓓ	16.	ⓐ ⓑ ⓒ ⓓ	25.	ⓐ ⓑ ⓒ ⓓ	34.	ⓐ ⓑ ⓒ ⓓ	43.	ⓐ ⓑ ⓒ ⓓ		
8.	ⓐ ⓑ ⓒ ⓓ	17.	ⓐ ⓑ ⓒ ⓓ	26.	ⓐ ⓑ ⓒ ⓓ	35.	ⓐ ⓑ ⓒ ⓓ	44.	ⓐ ⓑ ⓒ ⓓ		
9.	ⓐ ⓑ ⓒ ⓓ	18.	ⓐ ⓑ ⓒ ⓓ	27.	ⓐ ⓑ ⓒ ⓓ	36.	ⓐ ⓑ ⓒ ⓓ	45.	ⓐ ⓑ ⓒ ⓓ		

Practice Set 02

Time : 60 Mins. Max. Marks : 60

General Instructions

1. This question paper contains 50 questions.
2. All questions are compulsory. There is no negative marking.
3. Q. No. 1 to 40 are of 1 mark each and Q. No. 41 to 50 are of 2 marks each.
4. Use HB pencil / Blue ball point pen to mark your choice of answer by darkening the circles on the OMR Sheet.

MCQs 1 Mark Questions

1. Which city was/were established on the banks of Ganga river in the ancient period?
(a) Vindhyas
(b) Magadha
(c) Both (a) and (b)
(d) None of the above

2. Inamgaon is located in which of the following states of India, which is a site on the river Ghod, a tributary of the Bhima?
(a) Gujarat (b) Punjab
(c) Maharashtra (d) Rajasthan

3. The Pole Star indicates the direction to the ……… . It always remains in the same position in the sky.
(a) South (b) North
(c) East (d) West

4. Who among the following stated that 'the Earth is round and rotates on its own axis'?
(a) Varahamihira
(b) Bhaskara II
(c) Aryabhatta
(d) Brahmagupta

5. Sundarbans is the largest delta in the world. It is formed by which of the following rivers?
(a) The Ganga river
(b) The Brahmaputra river
(c) The Mahanadi river
(d) Both (a) and (b)

6. Which award is given to panchs for the excellent work done by them in the Panchayat?
(a) Bharat Ratna
(b) Nobel Prize
(c) Oscar
(d) Nirmal Gram Puruskar

7. Which among the following lays down the basic rules that have to be followed by everyone.
(a) Parliament (b) Constitution
(c) Court (d) Law

8. What is/are the feature(s) of Great Bath?
(a) It was made up of baked bricks.
(b) There were rooms from all sides.
(c) It is located in the Citadel of Mohenjo-daro.
(d) All of the above

9. Who among the following was author of the book 'The Discovery of India'?
(a) Mahatma Gandhi
(b) Jawaharlal Nehru
(c) Bal Gangadhar Tilak
(d) Gopal Krishna Gokhle

10. Complete the given analogy.
Prime Meridian : 0° longitude : : Equator : ?
(a) 1° latitude
(b) 1° longitude
(c) 0° degree latitude
(d) 3° latitude

11. Identify the main crop of village Kalpattu.
(a) Wheat (b) Sweet corn
(c) Paddy (d) Sugarcane

12. It is an old inscription which was found in Kandahar, present day Afghanistan, dates back to 2250 years ago. It was inscribed on the orders of Ashoka, ruler of Indian sub-continent. Identify the language which was used at the top of this inscription.

(a) Greek (b) Aramic
(c) Parsi (d) Prakrit

13. Mauna Kea (Hawaii) is an undersea mountain. It is located in which of the following oceans?
(a) The Indian Ocean (b) The Pacific Ocean
(c) Southern Ocean (d) The Arctic Ocean

14. Identify the gas which is the major constituent of the atmosphere by its percentage.
(a) Carbon monoxide
(b) Oxygen
(c) Carbon dioxide
(d) Nitrogen

15. What were the activities that the people of lower caste were not allowed to do in the early Indian society?
(a) Enter the temples
(b) Sit with upper caste's child in schools
(c) Take water from village well
(d) All of the above

16. Who among the following elect(s) the Panchayat head?
(a) Villagers
(b) Secretary
(c) All members of Gram Sabha
(d) All of the above

17. Which of the following is/are example(s) of Mahajanpadas?
(a) Magadha
(b) Avanti
(c) Kamboja
(d) All of the above

18. Which cities of Indus Valley had elaborate storehouses?
(a) Harappa
(b) Lothal
(c) Mohenjodaro
(d) All of the above

19. Identify the incorrect statement.
(a) Sun is a star.
(b) All objects shining in night sky are called celestial bodies.
(c) The pole star indicates South direction.
(d) None of the above

20. In which form of government, the King or Queen has the power to make decisions and run the government?
(a) Democracy (b) Socialism
(c) Monarchy (d) Oligarchy

21. Who have found the evidence of ancient farmers and herders from historical sites?
(a) Astrologists (b) Archaeologists
(c) Biologists (d) Historians

22. Identify the incorrectly matched pair.
(a) Earth – 1 Moon
(b) Mars – 2 Moons
(c) Mercury – 2 Moons
(d) Jupiter – 53 Moons

23. Who was the first person to step on the surface of the Moon?
(a) Neil Armstrong
(b) Rakesh Sharma
(c) Michael Collius
(d) Alan Shepard

24. What is the official language of South Africa which is also the first language of the South Africans?
(a) Zulu (b) Persian
(c) Sanskrit (d) English

25. Who among the following had a deep desire to learn about reality and was accepted as a student by a Brahmin teacher named Gautama?
(a) Satyakama Jabala
(b) Kishagotami
(c) Shankaracharya
(d) Both (a) and (b)

26. Who among the following was the famous ruler of a dynasty known as Guptas?
(a) Chandragupta (b) Samudragupta
(c) Ashoka (d) Siddhartha

27. It is an iron pillar which is located in Mehrauli, Delhi. It was built by which of the following rulers of the Indian sub-continent?

(a) Ashoka (b) Bindusara
(c) Chandragupta II (d) Samudragupta

28. Identify the type of maps which focus on specific information such as road, forests, industries, etc.
(a) Political maps (b) Thematic maps
(c) Physical maps (d) Topographic maps

29. Which of the following is/are associated with prejudice, that has become a common practice in Indian society?
(a) People's religious beliefs
(b) The colour of people's skin
(c) The region they come from
(d) All of the above

30. What would happen if the Earth did not rotate?
(a) The portion of the Earth facing the Sun would always experience day, thus bringing continuous warmth to the region.
(b) The other half would remain in darkness and be freezing cold all the time.
(c) Life would not have been possible in such extreme conditions.
(d) All of the above

31. .... was probably one of the places where people learnt to grow barley and wheat, and rear sheep and goats for the first time during Harappan period.

(a) Koldihwa (Uttar Pradesh)
(b) Gufkral (Kashmir)
(c) Mehrgarh (Pakistan)
(d) Hallur (Andhra Pradesh)

32. Which of the following books is associated with Chanakya's ideas?

(a) Vinaya Pitaka (b) Mahabharata
(c) Arthashastra (d) None of these

33. What is/are the purpose(s) of using magnetic Compass?

(a) For measuring distance
(b) For showing symbols
(c) For finding the directions
(d) All of the above

34. People of which community belongs to Nagaland?

(a) Angami (b) Chakhesang
(c) Konyak (d) Sangtam

35. Which region produces the Pushmina wool, which is considered very expensive?

(a) Jamshedpur (b) Kolkata
(c) Ladakh (d) Delhi

36. It is a fact that the mid-day Sun never shines overhead on any latitude beyond the ....

(a) Tropic of Cancer (b) Tropic of Capricorn
(c) Arctic Circle (d) Both (a) and (b)

37. What is the feature of Northern Black Polished Ware?

(a) They were made by coal.
(b) They were made in the North.
(c) They had a shiny black surface.
(d) They were made by the first craftsperson of the time.

38. Identify the ocean which is flanked by the North and South America on the Western side, and Europe and Africa on the Eastern side.

(a) Indian Ocean (b) Atlantik Ocean
(c) Pacific Ocean (d) Arctic Ocean

39. Patwari is known by different names. The other name(s) of Patwari is/are ....

(a) Lekhpal (b) Karamchari
(c) Village officer (d) All of these

40. What are the tasks of a Municipal Corporation in a state?

(a) To run the schools (b) To run hospitals
(c) To maintain parks (d) All of these

MCQs 2 Marks Questions

41. Consider the following statements.

I. In ancient period, some of the Rajas were probably chosen by the jana, the people.
II. The Ashvamedha or horse sacrifice became a ritual to recognise men as Rajas.
III. The Raja was a central figure in these rituals.

Which of the given statements is/are correct?

(a) Only I (b) I and II
(c) II and III (d) All of these

42. Read the given statements and select which ones are true (T) and which ones are false (F).

I. Maps are drawings, which reduce the entire world or a part of it to fit on a sheet of paper.
II. Maps are drawn to reduced scales but this reduction is done very carefully, so that the distance between the places is real.

III. It can only be possible when a small distance on paper represents a large distance on the ground.

Codes

	I	II	III
(a)	F	F	T
(b)	T	F	T
(c)	T	T	F
(d)	T	T	T

43. There are two statements marked as Assertion (A) and Reason (R). Mark your answer as per the codes given below.

Assertion (A) Areas lying between the Arctic Circle and the North Pole in thc Northern Hemisphere, and the Antarctic Circle and the South Pole in the Southern Hemisphere are very cold.

Reason (R) In these areas, the Sun does not rise much above the horizon.

Codes

(a) Both A and R are true and R is the correct explanation of A

(b) Both A and R are true, but R is not the correct explanation of A

(c) A is true, but R is false

(d) A is false, but R is true

44. Read the given statements and select which ones are true (T) and which ones are false (F).

I. Prashastis mention the ancestors of rulers.

II. Samudragupta's prashasti mentions his great grandfather, grandfather, father and mother.

III. Samudragupta's mother, Kumara Devi, belonged to the Lichchhavi gana, while his father, Chandragupta was the first ruler of the Gupta dynasty to adopt the grand title of Maharaj-Adhiraja.

IV. Samudragupta also used the title Maharaj-Adhiraja.

Codes

	I	II	III	IV
(a)	T	T	F	T
(b)	T	T	T	T
(c)	F	T	F	T
(d)	F	F	T	T

45. Match the following.

List I	List II
A. Tropic of Cancer	1. 23½° N
B. Tropic of Capricorn	2. 23½° S
C. Arctic Circle	3. 66½° N
D. Antarctic Circle	4. 66½° S

Codes

	A	B	C	D
(a)	1	2	3	4
(b)	4	3	2	1
(c)	3	4	1	2
(d)	4	1	2	3

46. Consider the following statements.

I. All Indian states are divided into districts.

II. The head of Tehsil or Taluka is the district collector.

III. The Revenue officers of Tehsil are called Tehsildars.

Which of the above statements is/are correct?

(a) Only I

(b) I, II and III

(c) II and III

(d) I and III

47. There are two statements marked as Assertion (A) and Reason (R). Mark your answer as per the codes given below.

Assertion (A) The Panchayati Raj System is a process through which people participate in their own government.

Reason (R) In rural areas, the Gram Panchayat is the first tier or level of democratic government.

Codes

(a) Both A and R are true and R is the correct explanation of A

(b) Both A and R are true, but R is not the correct explanation of A

(c) A is true, but R is false

(d) A is false, but R is true

48. There are two statements marked as Assertion (A) and Reason (R). Mark your answer as per the codes given below.

Assertion (A) Measuring land and keeping land records is the main work of the Patwari.

Reason (R) The Patwari usually has ways of measuring agricultural fields.

Codes

(a) Both A and R are true and R is the correct explanation of A

(b) Both A and R are true, but R is not the correct explanation of A

(c) A is true, but R is false

(d) A is false, but R is true

49. Identify the ruler from the following information.

- He was the first emperor of the Maurya Empire in ancient India.
- He was a ruler of Iron Age South Asia who expanded a geographically extensive kingdom based on Magadha.

(a) Bindusara

(b) Chandragupta Maurya

(c) Vikramaditya

(d) Megasthenes

50. Identify the important Mahajanpadas marked as A and B on the given outline map of India.

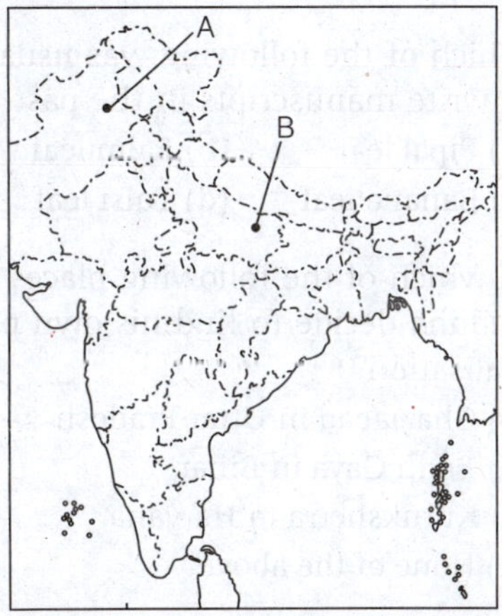

	A	B
(a)	Kosala	Avanti
(b)	Gandhara	Kosala
(c)	Kuru	Avanti
(d)	Hastinapur	Vaishali

Darken your choice with HB Pencil

1. ⓐ ⓑ ⓒ ⓓ	10. ⓐ ⓑ ⓒ ⓓ	19. ⓐ ⓑ ⓒ ⓓ	28. ⓐ ⓑ ⓒ ⓓ	37. ⓐ ⓑ ⓒ ⓓ	46. ⓐ ⓑ ⓒ ⓓ
2. ⓐ ⓑ ⓒ ⓓ	11. ⓐ ⓑ ⓒ ⓓ	20. ⓐ ⓑ ⓒ ⓓ	29. ⓐ ⓑ ⓒ ⓓ	38. ⓐ ⓑ ⓒ ⓓ	47. ⓐ ⓑ ⓒ ⓓ
3. ⓐ ⓑ ⓒ ⓓ	12. ⓐ ⓑ ⓒ ⓓ	21. ⓐ ⓑ ⓒ ⓓ	30. ⓐ ⓑ ⓒ ⓓ	39. ⓐ ⓑ ⓒ ⓓ	48. ⓐ ⓑ ⓒ ⓓ
4. ⓐ ⓑ ⓒ ⓓ	13. ⓐ ⓑ ⓒ ⓓ	22. ⓐ ⓑ ⓒ ⓓ	31. ⓐ ⓑ ⓒ ⓓ	40. ⓐ ⓑ ⓒ ⓓ	49. ⓐ ⓑ ⓒ ⓓ
5. ⓐ ⓑ ⓒ ⓓ	14. ⓐ ⓑ ⓒ ⓓ	23. ⓐ ⓑ ⓒ ⓓ	32. ⓐ ⓑ ⓒ ⓓ	41. ⓐ ⓑ ⓒ ⓓ	50. ⓐ ⓑ ⓒ ⓓ
6. ⓐ ⓑ ⓒ ⓓ	15. ⓐ ⓑ ⓒ ⓓ	24. ⓐ ⓑ ⓒ ⓓ	33. ⓐ ⓑ ⓒ ⓓ	42. ⓐ ⓑ ⓒ ⓓ	
7. ⓐ ⓑ ⓒ ⓓ	16. ⓐ ⓑ ⓒ ⓓ	25. ⓐ ⓑ ⓒ ⓓ	34. ⓐ ⓑ ⓒ ⓓ	43. ⓐ ⓑ ⓒ ⓓ	
8. ⓐ ⓑ ⓒ ⓓ	17. ⓐ ⓑ ⓒ ⓓ	26. ⓐ ⓑ ⓒ ⓓ	35. ⓐ ⓑ ⓒ ⓓ	44. ⓐ ⓑ ⓒ ⓓ	
9. ⓐ ⓑ ⓒ ⓓ	18. ⓐ ⓑ ⓒ ⓓ	27. ⓐ ⓑ ⓒ ⓓ	36. ⓐ ⓑ ⓒ ⓓ	45. ⓐ ⓑ ⓒ ⓓ	

Practice Set 03

Time : 60 Mins. Max. Marks : 60

General Instructions

1. This question paper contains 50 questions.
2. All questions are compulsory. There is no negative marking.
3. Q. No. 1 to 40 are of 1 mark each and Q. No. 41 to 50 are of 2 marks each.
4. Use HB pencil / Blue ball point pen to mark your choice of answer by darkening the circles on the OMR Sheet.

MCQs 1 Mark Questions

1. Which of the following was usually used to write manuscripts in the past time?

(a) Pipal leaf (b) Palm leaf
(c) Banana leaf (d) Tulsi leaf

2. In which of the following places did Buddha decide to find his own path to realisation?

(a) Ghaziabad in Uttar Pradesh
(b) Bodh Gaya in Bihar
(c) Kurukshetra in Haryana
(d) None of the above

3. Grid is a network of ...., which is/are used to locate any point on the globe very easily.

(a) parallels of latitudes and meridians of longitudes
(b) the Tropic of Cancer and the Tropic of Capricorn
(c) the North pole and the South pole
(d) All of the above

4. Who among the following composed a famous Tamil epic, the Silappadikaram, around 1800 years ago?

(a) Kalhana (b) Kalidasa
(c) Ilango (d) Kabir Das

5. Where do the rivers Mahanadi, Godavari, Krishna and Kaveri drain?

(a) Western Ghats
(b) Lakshadweep
(c) Bay of Bengal
(d) Arabian Sea

6. Which of the following is not an example of geographical diversity in India?

(a) India is geographically divided into four parts.
(b) India is a vast country.
(c) There are many numbers of races in India.
(d) None of the above

7. Which of the following is not a job of Municipal Corporation?

(a) To keep the streets and markets clean.
(b) To construct gardens and maintains them.
(c) To build hotels for the tourists.
(d) To run schools, hospitals and dispensaries.

8. Pit houses were found at which site?

(a) Inamgaon
(b) Burzahom
(c) Bhimbetka
(d) Kurnool

9. In what way(s) the ancient coins were different from the ones we use today?
(a) Coins were made of stones
(b) Coins were made of baked clay
(c) Coins were made of bones
(d) All of the above

10. Maps use different colours to show different features. Yellow colour is particularly used for which of the following features?
(a) Plateaus (b) Water bodies
(c) Mountains (d) Plants

11. The Ward Panchs and the Sarpanch form the Gram Panchayat. The Gram Panchayat is elected for .... years.
(a) five (b) six
(c) seven (d) ten

12. .... is a centralised office that deals with problems and questions that consumers/ customers have regarding goods purchased and services like banking, ticket booking, etc.
(a) Customer Care Service
(b) Call Centre
(c) Both (a) and (b)
(d) None of the above

13. The given below picture shows a geographical phenomenon. Identify it.

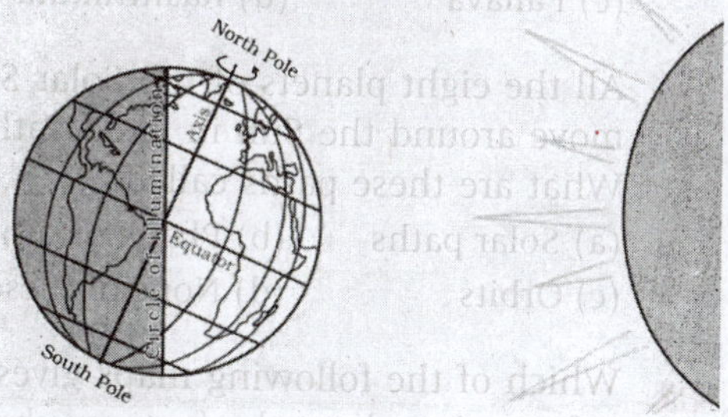

(a) Revolution of the Earth
(b) Day and night on the Earth due to rotation
(c) Circle of illumination
(d) Both (b) and (c)

14. What were the different ways in which grain was used in the past time?
(a) As food (b) As gifts
(c) Stored for food (d) All of these

15. What is the best means of measuring time?
(a) Movement of the Moon
(b) Movement of the Planets
(c) Movement of the Earth
(d) All of the above

16. How much time does the Earth take to revolve around the Sun?
(a) $365\frac{1}{4}$ days (b) 360 days
(c) 24 hours (d) 365 days

17. A struggle of women got strengthened during the First World War which is called the Women's Suffrage Movement. The term 'suffrage' usually means ....
(a) Right to Liberty
(b) Right to Speech
(c) Right to Work
(d) Right to Vote

18. What was/were the restrictions imposed on the untouchable group of people?
(a) Untouchable group of people was denied education.
(b) Untouchable group of people was denied to transport and medical facilities.
(c) Untouchable group of people was denied to offer prayers.
(d) All of the above

19. The .... was built on a raised ground and high walls made of bricks.
(a) Manuscripts
(b) Citadel
(c) Both (a) and (b)
(d) Burials

20. Puhar or Kaveripattinam was an important port of which of the following chiefs during ancient period?

(a) Cheras (b) Pandyas
(c) Cholas (d) None of these

21. A type of classification is represented in the given picture. Identify the domain name of classification.

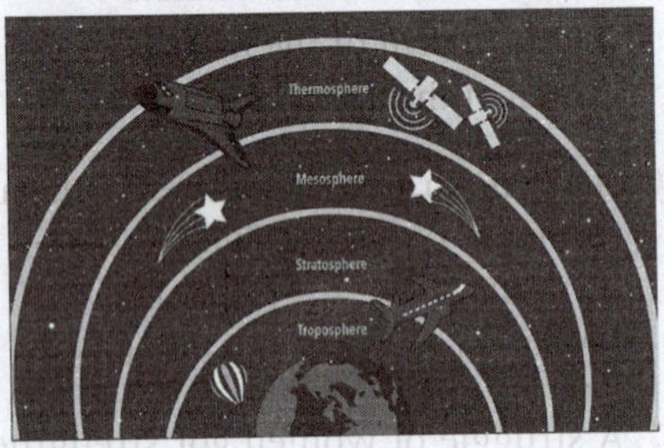

(a) Layers of atmosphere
(b) Layers of lithosphere
(c) Layers of hydrosphere
(d) None of the above

22. The citizens of India have the right to approach the .... if they feel there is violation of any law by an individual or by the government.

(a) Upper house (b) Parliament
(c) Court (d) Lawyer

23. South African people were divided into which of the following groups?

(a) South Africans, black, Indian and coloured races
(b) White, Indians and coloured races
(c) White, black, Indian and coloured races
(d) White, black and Americans

24. Which types of plants is/are select in the process of domestication?

(a) Plants that yield large-size grain
(b) Plants that have strong stalks
(c) Plants that are capable of bearing the weight of the ripe grain
(d) All of the above

25. What term is used for large landowners in the Tamil region?

(a) Vellalar (b) Uzhavar
(c) Kadaisiyar (d) Adimai

26. Which of the following is correct about outer planets?

(a) They are made up of rocks.
(b) Marks, Jupiter, Saturn are outer planets.
(c) These planets are small in size.
(d) They are made up of gaseous and liquids.

27. Which of the following is/are a non-form activity?

(a) Basket making (b) Weaving
(c) Barber (d) All of these

28. Revenue officer comes under the District Collector. She/He is also known as ....

(a) SHO
(b) Tehsildar
(c) Patwari
(d) Sub Divisional Magistrate

29. The kingdom of which dynasty was centred around the Raichur Doab, between the Krishna and Tungabhadra rivers?

(a) Satavahana (b) Chalukya
(c) Pallava (d) Rashtrakuta

30. All the eight planets of the Solar System move around the Sun in fixed paths. What are these paths called?

(a) Solar paths (b) Planet's paths
(c) Orbits (d) None of these

31. Which of the following maps gives more information about the features shown on this map?

(a) Small scale map (b) Large scale map
(c) Ordinary map (d) None of these

32. It is a type of boat race which organises in this state during the festival of Onam. Identify the state from the following options.

(a) Manipur (b) Assam
(c) Kerala (d) Karnataka

33. Find the incorrect pair.

(a) Copper – Found in Rajasthan
(b) Tin – Found in Uttar Pradesh
(c) Gold – Found in Karnataka
(d) Precious stones – Found in Gujarat, Iran and Afghanistan

34. Consider the following statements about the Sun and choose the correct option.

(a) The Sun is in the centre of the Solar System.
(b) It provides the pulling force that binds the Solar System.
(c) The Sun is the ultimate source of heat and light for the Solar System.
(d) All of the above

35. India is surrounded by .... in the East.

(a) Bay of Bengal
(b) Himalayas
(c) Arabian Sea
(d) Indian ocean

36. The Sahara Desert, the world's largest hot desert, is located in this continent. The continent is bound on all sides by oceans and seas. Identify the continent.

(a) Asia (b) Europe
(c) Africa (d) South America

37. Which metal was/were mainly used to make most of the things found by the archaeologists in the Harappan cities?

(a) Stone
(b) Copper and Gold
(c) Silver
(d) All of the above

38. When members of the same family become rulers one after another, the family is often called a ....

(a) dynasty (b) reign
(c) clan (d) tribe

39. Arctic Ocean is connected with Pacific Ocean by which strait?

(a) Berring strait
(b) Palk strait
(c) Gibraltor strait
(d) Hormuz strait

40. Identify the religion that reached Tibet via Ladakh.

(a) Buddhism (b) Islam
(c) Jainism (d) Christianity

MCQs 2 Marks Questions

41. There are two statements marked as Assertion (A) and Reason (R). Mark your answer as per the codes given below.

Assertion (A) Ashoka was the only king who gave up conquest after winning a war.

Reason (R) Ashoka was horrified when he saw violence and bloodsheds.

Codes

(a) Both A and R are true and R is the correct explanation of A
(b) Both A and R are true, but R is not the correct explanation of A
(c) A is true, but R is false
(d) A is false, but R is true

42. Identify the personality from the following information.

- He was the third ruler of the Gupta Empire.
- He led an expedition to Western India and conquered the last of Shakas.

(a) Chandragupta II
(b) Ashoka
(c) Bindusara
(d) Chandragupta Maurya

43. Match the following.

List I	List II
A. Sukta	1. Hymns of Rigveda
B. Yajna	2. Sacrifice
C. Dasa	3. Slave
D. Megalith	4. Stone- boulder

Codes

	A	B	C	D		A	B	C	D
(a)	1	2	3	4	(b)	3	4	1	2
(c)	4	3	2	1	(d)	2	4	1	3

44. Consider the following statements.

I. Domestication was a gradual process that took place in many parts of the world. It began about 12,000 years ago.
II. Some of the earliest plants to be domesticated were wheat and barley.
III. The earliest domesticated animals include sheep and goat.

Which of the above statements is/are correct?

Codes

(a) Only I (b) I and II
(c) II and III (d) All of these

45. Read the following statements and select which ones are true (T) and which ones are false (F).

I. The Buddha encouraged animal sacrifices.
II. Sarnath is important because it was the place where the Buddha taught for the first time.
III. The Buddha attained enlightenment at Bodh Gaya.

Codes

	I	II	III		I	II	III
(a)	T	T	F	(b)	F	T	T
(c)	T	T	T	(d)	F	F	T

46. Read the following statements and select which ones are true (T) and which ones are false (F).

I. Kerala is a state in the South-West corner of India.
II. Kerala is surrounded by the sea on one side and hills on the other.
III. A number of spices like pepper, cloves and cardamoms are grown on the hills in the state.

Codes

	I	II	III		I	II	III
(a)	T	T	F	(b)	T	T	T
(c)	T	F	T	(d)	F	T	F

47. Consider the following statements.

I. Every village Panchayat is divided into wards, i.e. smaller areas.
II. The Gram Panchayat has a Secretary who is also the Secretary of the Gram Sabha.
III. The Secretary is not an elected person but it is appointed by the government.

Which of the above statements is/are correct?

(a) Only I (b) I and II
(c) II and III (d) All of these

48. There are two statements marked as Assertion (A) and Reason (R). Mark your answer as per the codes given below.

Assertion (A) The value of each latitude is followed by either the word North or South. Generally, this is indicated by the letter 'N' or 'S'.

Reason (R) All parallels North of the equator are called 'North latitudes.' Similarly, all parallels South of the equator are called 'South latitudes.'

Codes

(a) Both A and R are true and R is the correct explanation of A

(b) Both A and R are true, but R is not the correct explanation of A

(c) A is true, but R is false

(d) A is false, but R is true

49. Identify the mountain ranges marked as A and B on the given outline map of the world

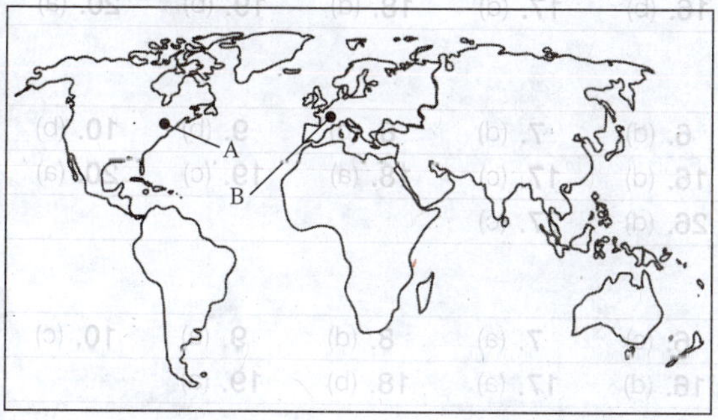

	A	B
(a)	Alpes	The Himalaya Mountains
(b)	Appalachian Mountains	Alpes
(c)	Rocky Mountains	Drakensberg Mountains
(d)	Atlas Mountains	Rocky Mountains

50. There are two statements marked as Assertion (A) and Reason (R). Mark your answer as per the codes given below.

Assertion (A) The Sun is our nearest star, but its tremendous heat is not felt so much by us.

Reason (R) The Sun is far away from the Earth about 150 million km away.

Codes

(a) Both A and R are true and R is the correct explanation of A

(b) Both A and R are true, but R is not the correct explanation of A

(c) A is true, but R is false

(d) A is false, but R is true

Darken your choice with HB Pencil

1.	ⓐ ⓑ ⓒ ⓓ	10.	ⓐ ⓑ ⓒ ⓓ	19.	ⓐ ⓑ ⓒ ⓓ	28.	ⓐ ⓑ ⓒ ⓓ	37.	ⓐ ⓑ ⓒ ⓓ	46.	ⓐ ⓑ ⓒ ⓓ
2.	ⓐ ⓑ ⓒ ⓓ	11.	ⓐ ⓑ ⓒ ⓓ	20.	ⓐ ⓑ ⓒ ⓓ	29.	ⓐ ⓑ ⓒ ⓓ	38.	ⓐ ⓑ ⓒ ⓓ	47.	ⓐ ⓑ ⓒ ⓓ
3.	ⓐ ⓑ ⓒ ⓓ	12.	ⓐ ⓑ ⓒ ⓓ	21.	ⓐ ⓑ ⓒ ⓓ	30.	ⓐ ⓑ ⓒ ⓓ	39.	ⓐ ⓑ ⓒ ⓓ	48.	ⓐ ⓑ ⓒ ⓓ
4.	ⓐ ⓑ ⓒ ⓓ	13.	ⓐ ⓑ ⓒ ⓓ	22.	ⓐ ⓑ ⓒ ⓓ	31.	ⓐ ⓑ ⓒ ⓓ	40.	ⓐ ⓑ ⓒ ⓓ	49.	ⓐ ⓑ ⓒ ⓓ
5.	ⓐ ⓑ ⓒ ⓓ	14.	ⓐ ⓑ ⓒ ⓓ	23.	ⓐ ⓑ ⓒ ⓓ	32.	ⓐ ⓑ ⓒ ⓓ	41.	ⓐ ⓑ ⓒ ⓓ	50.	ⓐ ⓑ ⓒ ⓓ
6.	ⓐ ⓑ ⓒ ⓓ	15.	ⓐ ⓑ ⓒ ⓓ	24.	ⓐ ⓑ ⓒ ⓓ	33.	ⓐ ⓑ ⓒ ⓓ	42.	ⓐ ⓑ ⓒ ⓓ		
7.	ⓐ ⓑ ⓒ ⓓ	16.	ⓐ ⓑ ⓒ ⓓ	25.	ⓐ ⓑ ⓒ ⓓ	34.	ⓐ ⓑ ⓒ ⓓ	43.	ⓐ ⓑ ⓒ ⓓ		
8.	ⓐ ⓑ ⓒ ⓓ	17.	ⓐ ⓑ ⓒ ⓓ	26.	ⓐ ⓑ ⓒ ⓓ	35.	ⓐ ⓑ ⓒ ⓓ	44.	ⓐ ⓑ ⓒ ⓓ		
9.	ⓐ ⓑ ⓒ ⓓ	18.	ⓐ ⓑ ⓒ ⓓ	27.	ⓐ ⓑ ⓒ ⓓ	36.	ⓐ ⓑ ⓒ ⓓ	45.	ⓐ ⓑ ⓒ ⓓ		

Answer Sheet

Chapter 01

1. (a)	2. (c)	3. (b)	4. (d)	5. (b)	6. (d)	7. (d)	8. (c)	9. (a)	10. (b)
11. (d)	12. (d)	13. (d)	14. (c)	15. (a)	16. (b)	17. (a)	18. (a)	19. (c)	20. (d)
21. (c)	22. (a)	23. (a)							

Chapter 02

1. (b)	2. (d)	3. (d)	4. (c)	5. (a)	6. (a)	7. (b)	8. (a)	9. (d)	10. (b)
11. (a)	12. (d)	13. (a)	14. (d)	15. (a)	16. (b)	17. (a)	18. (d)	19. (c)	20. (a)
21. (a)	22. (b)	23. (c)							

Chapter 03

1. (b)	2. (b)	3. (c)	4. (d)	5. (c)	6. (d)	7. (c)	8. (d)	9. (b)	10. (a)
11. (a)	12. (b)	13. (c)	14. (a)	15. (c)	16. (b)	17. (d)	18. (d)	19. (b)	20. (a)

Chapter 04

1. (a)	2. (a)	3. (d)	4. (c)	5. (b)	6. (d)	7. (d)	8. (b)	9. (b)	10. (b)
11. (c)	12. (c)	13. (a)	14. (a)	15. (c)	16. (d)	17. (c)	18. (a)	19. (c)	20. (a)
21. (a)	22. (b)	23. (b)	24. (a)	25. (a)	26. (d)	27. (c)			

Chapter 05

1. (b)	2. (b)	3. (b)	4. (c)	5. (b)	6. (c)	7. (a)	8. (d)	9. (a)	10. (c)
11. (d)	12. (a)	13. (b)	14. (c)	15. (c)	16. (d)	17. (a)	18. (b)	19. (a)	

Chapter 06

1. (a)	2. (a)	3. (c)	4. (b)	5. (a)	6. (b)	7. (c)	8. (a)	9. (d)	10. (c)
11. (b)	12. (d)	13. (a)	14. (d)	15. (c)	16. (a)	17. (a)	18. (c)	19. (c)	20. (d)
21. (d)	22. (a)	23. (d)	24. (b)	25. (a)	26. (c)				

Chapter 07

1. (a)	2. (b)	3. (b)	4. (a)	5. (d)	6. (d)	7. (b)	8. (a)	9. (c)	10. (a)
11. (b)	12. (c)	13. (c)	14. (c)	15. (a)	16. (a)	17. (d)	18. (b)	19. (d)	20. (b)
21. (a)	22. (b)	23. (c)	24. (d)	25. (a)					

Chapter 08

1. (b)	2. (d)	3. (c)	4. (a)	5. (b)	6. (d)	7. (b)	8. (a)	9. (b)	10. (d)
11. (d)	12. (d)	13. (a)	14. (c)	15. (a)	16. (a)	17. (d)	18. (a)	19. (b)	20. (b)
21. (a)	22. (a)	23. (b)	24. (c)	25. (b)	26. (a)	27. (a)	28. (d)		

Chapter 09

1. (b)	2. (c)	3. (a)	4. (c)	5. (a)	6. (a)	7. (b)	8. (a)	9. (c)	10. (d)
11. (a)	12. (c)	13. (c)	14. (c)	15. (b)	16. (c)	17. (a)	18. (b)	19. (a)	20. (d)
21. (d)	22. (b)	23. (c)	24. (b)						

Chapter 10

1. (a) 2. (c) 3. (b) 4. (b) 5. (b) 6. (a) 7. (c) 8. (d) 9. (c) 10. (b)
11. (c) 12. (a) 13. (a) 14. (c) 15. (b) 16. (b) 17. (d) 18. (d) 19. (c) 20. (a)
21. (b) 22. (c) 23. (b) 24. (b) 25. (c)

Chapter 11

1. (b) 2. (d) 3. (a) 4. (d) 5. (b) 6. (a) 7. (a) 8. (c) 9. (b) 10. (d)
11. (c) 12. (c) 13. (d) 14. (a) 15. (b) 16. (a) 17. (c) 18. (a) 19. (c) 20. (d)

Chapter 12

1. (d) 2. (b) 3. (a) 4. (c) 5. (c) 6. (c) 7. (d) 8. (c) 9. (c) 10. (c)
11. (c) 12. (c) 13. (b) 14. (a) 15. (b) 16. (a)

Chapter 13

1. (d) 2. (c) 3. (a) 4. (b) 5. (a) 6. (d) 7. (c) 8. (d) 9. (d) 10. (c)
11. (a) 12. (b) 13. (b) 14. (b) 15. (b) 16. (a) 17. (c) 18. (c)

Chapter 14

1. (c) 2. (a) 3. (b) 4. (a) 5. (c) 6. (b) 7. (c) 8. (b) 9. (a) 10. (d)
11. (b) 12. (c) 13. (a) 14. (a) 15. (b) 16. (b) 17. (a) 18. (b) 19. (c) 20. (a)
21. (b) 22. (c) 23. (a) 24. (b)

Chapter 15

1. (a) 2. (d) 3. (b) 4. (c) 5. (a) 6. (c) 7. (d) 8. (b) 9. (c) 10. (b)
11. (d) 12. (b) 13. (d) 14. (b) 15. (c)

Chapter 16

1. (a) 2. (c) 3. (a) 4. (c) 5. (c) 6. (d) 7. (c) 8. (a) 9. (a) 10. (c)
11. (a) 12. (b) 13. (b) 14. (b) 15. (b) 16. (b) 17. (c) 18. (c)

Chapter 17

1. (a) 2. (a) 3. (b) 4. (c) 5. (d) 6. (a) 7. (a) 8. (b) 9. (d) 10. (c)
11. (d) 12. (a) 13. (c) 14. (b) 15. (b) 16. (a) 17. (a) 18. (c) 19. (a) 20. (b)
21. (d) 22. (c) 23. (a) 24. (b)

Chapter 18

1. (c) 2. (c) 3. (d) 4. (b) 5. (c) 6. (d) 7. (d) 8. (b) 9. (a) 10. (c)
11. (c) 12. (b) 13. (a) 14. (d) 15. (b)

Practice Set 01

1. (b)	**2.** (c)	**3.** (c)	**4.** (c)	**5.** (d)	**6.** (c)	**7.** (b)	**8.** (c)	**9.** (c)	**10.** (b)
11. (b)	**12.** (b)	**13.** (d)	**14.** (b)	**15.** (d)	**16.** (b)	**17.** (a)	**18.** (a)	**19.** (c)	**20.** (c)
21. (d)	**22.** (d)	**23.** (c)	**24.** (d)	**25.** (c)	**26.** (c)	**27.** (c)	**28.** (c)	**29.** (c)	**30.** (b)
31. (c)	**32.** (b)	**33.** (c)	**34.** (d)	**35.** (b)	**36.** (c)	**37.** (b)	**38.** (d)	**39.** (c)	**40.** (b)
41. (a)	**42.** (c)	**43.** (b)	**44.** (d)	**45.** (a)	**46.** (d)	**47.** (b)	**48.** (a)	**49.** (b)	**50.** (d)

Practice Set 02

1. (b)	**2.** (c)	**3.** (b)	**4.** (c)	**5.** (d)	**6.** (d)	**7.** (b)	**8.** (d)	**9.** (b)	**10.** (c)
11. (c)	**12.** (b)	**13.** (b)	**14.** (d)	**15.** (d)	**16.** (c)	**17.** (d)	**18.** (d)	**19.** (c)	**20.** (c)
21. (b)	**22.** (c)	**23.** (a)	**24.** (a)	**25.** (a)	**26.** (b)	**27.** (c)	**28.** (b)	**29.** (d)	**30.** (d)
31. (c)	**32.** (c)	**33.** (c)	**34.** (b)	**35.** (c)	**36.** (d)	**37.** (c)	**38.** (b)	**39.** (d)	**40.** (d)
41. (d)	**42.** (d)	**43.** (a)	**44.** (b)	**45.** (a)	**46.** (c)	**47.** (b)	**48.** (b)	**49.** (b)	**50.** (b)

Practice Set 03

1. (b)	**2.** (b)	**3.** (a)	**4.** (c)	**5.** (c)	**6.** (c)	**7.** (c)	**8.** (b)	**9.** (d)	**10.** (a)
11. (a)	**12.** (b)	**13.** (d)	**14.** (d)	**15.** (d)	**16.** (a)	**17.** (d)	**18.** (d)	**19.** (b)	**20.** (c)
21. (a)	**22.** (c)	**23.** (c)	**24.** (d)	**25.** (a)	**26.** (d)	**27.** (d)	**28.** (b)	**29.** (b)	**30.** (c)
31. (b)	**32.** (c)	**33.** (b)	**34.** (d)	**35.** (a)	**36.** (c)	**37.** (d)	**38.** (a)	**39.** (a)	**40.** (a)
41. (a)	**42.** (a)	**43.** (a)	**44.** (b)	**45.** (b)	**46.** (b)	**47.** (d)	**48.** (a)	**49.** (b)	**50.** (a)